Transnational Korean Television

Transnational Communication and Critical/Cultural Studies

Series Editor: Ahmet Atay, the College of Wooster

The goal of this interdisciplinary series is to connect communication and critical/cultural studies by featuring critical inquiry that focuses on economic, cultural, social, and political practices in everyday life and mediated texts. However, this critical inquiry and analysis employ the standpoint of communication. This series will promote critical analysis and reflection on important social and cultural issues, including diversity, reflexivity, political systems, gender, race/ethnicity, sexuality/gender issues, class, ability, nationalism, globalization, postcolonialism, immigration, and youth.

Books in this series represent academic rigor, rhetorical self-reflexivity, methodological and theoretical innovations, and thematic and topical relevance in their orientation. They will analyze historical and contemporary culture; cultural, social, economic, and material conditions; power dynamics within local, national, and global cultures and social institutions; practices of resistance, cultural re-appropriation, and social justice; and cultural, social, material, political, and economic dimensions of everyday life.

Scholars who can address these issues will offer international and global perspectives. This series invites critical inquiry into the concepts of power, hegemony, agency, identity, cultural/social change, and social justice in cultural practices. It is open to contributions from scholars working within qualitative and critical/cultural methods (including ethnographic methods, performance, narrative, and textual and discourse analysis), as well as scholars working in sexuality/gender/queer studies, race studies, globalization, postcolonial studies, ethnographic methods, visual culture studies, media studies, and film studies insofar as their research intersects with communication and cultural studies.

Recent Titles in This Series

Transnational Korean Television: Cultural Storytelling and Digital Audiences
By Hyejung Ju
Planting the Future: The Rhetorical Legacy of Wangari Maathai
Edited by Eddah M. Mutua, Alberto González, and Anke Wolbert

Transnational Korean Television

Cultural Storytelling and Digital Audiences

Hyejung Ju

LEXINGTON BOOKS
Lanham • Boulder • New York • London

Published by Lexington Books
An imprint of The Rowman & Littlefield Publishing Group, Inc.
4501 Forbes Boulevard, Suite 200, Lanham, Maryland 20706
www.rowman.com

6 Tinworth Street, London SE11 5AL, United Kingdom

Copyright © 2020 by The Rowman & Littlefield Publishing Group, Inc.

All rights reserved. No part of this book may be reproduced in any form or by any electronic or mechanical means, including information storage and retrieval systems, without written permission from the publisher, except by a reviewer who may quote passages in a review.

British Library Cataloguing in Publication Information Available

Library of Congress Control Number: 2019950877
ISBN 978-1-4985-6517-2 (cloth)
ISBN 978-1-4985-6519-6 (pbk)
ISBN 978-1-4985-6518-9 (electronic)

Contents

List of Figures and Tables   vii

Introduction   1

PART I: TRANSNATIONAL KOREAN TELEVISION WITH EAST ASIA   7

1   Transforming the Korean Television Industry: The Korean Wave   9

2   Korean TV Drama Narratives: Are Korean Dramas a Transcultural Story?   27

3   Korean TV Shows with East Asian Partnership   45

PART II: TRANSNATIONAL KOREAN TELEVISION IN AMERICA   61

4   Digital Audiences, Fans, and Fandom   63

5   The Power of Streaming TV: Netflix, DramaFever, and American Viewers   79

6   Korean Television Formats   95

Conclusion   111

Bibliography   117

Index   129

About the Author   131

List of Figures and Tables

FIGURES

Figure 1.1	Korean TV Program Exports by Annual Revenues.	19
Figure 1.2	Korean TV Program Exports by Genre (2015).	20
Figure 2.1	The Scene for a Romance Narrative: Sharing an Umbrella.	37
Figure 2.2	A Scene from a Romance Narrative: *Secret Garden*.	39
Figure 3.1	*Boys Over Flowers* (Korea).	48
Figure 5.1	Netflix's Korean TV Shows.	89
Figure 6.1	Scene: Saving a Kid's Life in *The Good Doctor*—Original Korean Drama versus the U.S. Remake.	106

TABLES

Table 6.1	Korean TV Format Trade: TV Drama Series	101
Table 6.2	Korean TV Format Trade: Variety Shows	107

Introduction

As digitalization and globalization transform our relationships with media, particularly television, the quantity, quality, and diversity of audiovisual content on television are increasingly connected in transnational and transcultural contexts. Television viewers' navigation of digital media platforms brings up new patterns to receive and entertain with different kinds of TV stories produced overseas. For example, the capacity of video-sharing technology, such as YouTube, allows individuals to voluntarily reproduce foreign TV shows as self-edited new videos with local language subtitles in the hopes for sharing them broadly with other sympathized fans. In the United States, the foreign TV show viewership has demonstrated an increase with the online streaming (Lobato 2018; McDonald and Smith-Rowsey 2016), which gives television viewers frequent and easy access to numerous TV shows produced abroad.

The spread of South Korean popular culture (hereafter, Korean) internationally, especially Korean television drama and K-pop, is now well-documented and frequently observed within Asia and beyond. Since 2010, this transnational flow of Korean media and pop culture into the Western cultural bloc has been more visible, including the United Kingdom and the United States, so this new tendency draws a sharp attention among Western media industries. In the Western world, increasing viewership and fandoms for both Korean television dramas (K-drama) and Korean pop music (K-pop) are eye opening, yet, certainly unusual phenomena at the same time. The notion of *flow* in the global media emerged in the 1970s, and has been used by broadcasting industry distributors and media scholars in at least two distinct ways (White 2003). In definition, *flow*, first, refers to the planned sequence in which segments or strips of TV programming unfold onscreen (Harrington and Bielby 2005), as seen from a narrow industrial view. Second, but more broadly, *flow* refers to the mobility of both finished TV programs and

TV formats in international media marketplaces. The latter concept of *flow* has been developed in global media studies as media scholars have investigated different border-crossing media streams on national and regional levels to explore the transnational and global circulation of TV programs in foreign origins. As such, today's outbound path of Korean television programs ties with this second definition of *flow*. In the line of Korean Wave studies over the years, the empirical cases of Korean media flows demonstrate a variety of Korean media and pop content inclusion, such as K-drama series, K-pop, movies, online games, beauty items, fashion commodities, and foods. With this in mind, this book focuses especially on articulating the Korean media flows in light of transnational television flows on the verge of its acerbated mobility overseas in both the Eastern and Western cultural marketplaces. Based on the expand scope, visibility, and continuity of the Korean Wave today, this often accounts for a contraflow case in comparison to the Western media and pop culture flow as central transnational media flows across the world.

More importantly, the Korean Wave for the past two decades has been experiencing continuities and discontinuities in its popularity cycles, key content, the speed of and scope of distribution, but at the beginning of the 2010s, this came to new and more visible inflows to the Western entertainment industries and markets thanks to the rapid surge of K-pop. For sure, K-pop's current global popularity seems larger than the former impact of the Korean Wave around the world compared to the Asia-centered Korean TV dramas' huge popularity a few years ago. However, it is worth noting that Korean TV dramas still remain as another key content circulated and consumed well among the Western cultural consumers and audiences. In other words, Korean TV dramas opened the overseas flow of the original Korean media content at first and since then they contribute largely to attracting many transnational television viewers and fans; now this contribution keeps reaching out more to Western audiences passing over Asian audiences. Along with the K-pop's popularity, Korean TV dramas have extended its promotional paths of distribution and consumption in the brand-new television and entertainment markets, enabling more Western audiences to be familiar with other types of Korean media and pop content.

In media scholarship, a body of studies on the Korean Wave has tended to map out the former and present Korean media's transnational flows relying on a few theories of cultural globalization. These scholarly discourses on both Korean Wave and the related phenomena produce a wide and/or diverse theoretical approach by embracing either critical transnational culture or media globalization framework. Despite of theoretical diversity in the Korean Wave discourses, this does answer only partial inquiries of to what extent Korean media's flows overseas has been influenced by geo-cultural media boundaries and the predominant industrial pecking orders. However, the pace, scope, variety, and magnitude of transnational Korean media flows in a significant pinpoint do not remain in the same environments as well as conditions over the years, as likewise the wave was happened in the beginning. Thus, it is certainly important to reveal how the very recent transnational circulation of Korean television drives not only the flow of various kinds of content and formats, but also reciprocal interchanges of diverse levels of human, financial, technological, and cultural elements. This nature suggests a reconstruction of Korean Wave discussions in academia, and mostly requires high demand of sharp insights on the entangled meanings of the growing transnational Korean television broadly more on the Western mediascapes.

Taken all together in this book, I aim to provide a comprehensive analysis about the recent transnational flow of Korean television to the U.S. television as well as their audiences, including an analysis on online viewership through streaming TV services such as Netflix. I suggest three reasons why this book delves into the discussion specifically about Korean television programs' in America over its impact within Asia. First, Korean television programs (especially Korean TV dramas) nowadays enter into America and demonstrates its consumption by different audience groups; certainly this is a very rare case that a non-Western television program broadcast and remade in American television. Understanding this emerging trend can contribute to enriching and verifying the theoretical notion of transnational Korean media flows beyond established scholarly arguments. Also, this clarification can reexamine and reconsider the uneven phase of television program trades for many years between the United States and Korea under East-West dyad of global media and culture industry. While the presence of television programs from Japan and China had already been established in the United States, these were mainly assisted by video distribution networks mainly targeting diasporas' community members to feed desire for their cultural origins. However, Korean television dramas as the domestic cultural form that being consumed by different transnational television viewers, including the U.S. viewers, as such a different level of growth, cultural and technological conditions bring little scholarly work toward essential content values and uniqueness as a non-Western media form.

Second, some scholars have simply concluded that the current success of Korean television dramas in international markets attributed to the Korean government's economic engineering to commodify the entire country's media as an export brand (Artz 2015). On the one hand, it is an insight; but on the other side, it is too much of a simplification when seeking to understand this increasing contraflow by non-Western national television in border-crossing contexts. Moreover, this doesn't probe to the actual influence for transnational flows of Korean television to the U.S. media and audience, given the changing trade structure and convergent technologies for television entertainment in the global mediascape. The suggested governmental intervention in Korean television outflows claims an emphasis on a national support of domestic media systems, and yet, many television systems in varying degrees are still keen on a national operation while managing a global drive at the same time. In other words, television, the medium itself, has relied heavily on a national boundary. Again, the suggested explanation for transnational Korean television has missed the factual and vital changes of the global media and industry alongside numerous marginal or small scopes of national media systems.

Third, the existing scholarly work and the media industries' reports tell us little about how to attract and motivate U.S. audiences to consume transnational Korean television dramas among other foreign TV show counterparts. Through my former studies, it's been demonstrated that viewers as well as fans of Korean TV dramas experienced different modes of reception in association with elements of Korean drama narratives and ways of representation of the peculiar storyline. For example, the individual viewer's interview below shares the similar note in this token from Korean drama viewers in the United States:

> Joyce Brand (Female, 65, in LA) admits that she didn't know anything about South Korean television, until a serial popped up on her Netflix recommendation list. She said, "I started watching it, and as soon as I saw the subtitles, I thought about turning it off. But then I thought, well, I'll watch it for a few minutes, and within 10 minutes I was hooked. I watched the whole 20 hours." The show she was hooked is a Korean TV drama called *City Hunter*, which is a hit thriller about a man who's hunting down his father's killer. (Fujita 2014)

The interview above shows increasing interest to Korean TV dramas among U.S. audiences. However, little research has told about what and why those U.S. audiences are drawing much attention to unfamiliar Korean TV dramas. To delve into this influence in the U.S. television, the investigation to the dynamics of converging television technologies, television genres, needs of entertainment, and new market environment seems a high demand. In sync with the U.S. media's economic power driven by their multinational media ownerships in global markets, the case of Korean television into the United States (or more broadly, Western media markets) sheds light on the significant impact of rapidly growing grassroots control of television content via online and digital TV platforms relying on their free desire for revelation of a fresh content regardless of production origins. In the meantime transnational Korean television toward the United States and Europe, where had high cultural barriers to receive non-Western content, comes to an overturn of the former East-West media packing order within uneven industrial hierarchy. Beyond the market size, promotional power and advanced funding, digital television and its content flows apparently transform television consumption patterns by various grassroots' capability to pioneer new transnational and/or transcultural TV content.

As a preview, I divide this book into two primary subjects, to account for a breadth of transnational Korean television flows along with the Korean Wave; this aims to deepen the widespread discourses of the Korean Wave studies in several different approaches. Simultaneously, this geographical overview regarding the transnational Korean television turns discursive insights into the evolving phases of Korean television and broadcasting systems as the epicenter of the flow of Korean TV drama. In short, part I includes analyses of the Korean television system, the meanings of Korean TV dramas pertaining the Korean Wave phenomena, regional functions of Korean television in Asian mediascapes, and the quintessential storytelling and structure of Korean drama narratives that incur participatory consumption among transnational audiences. In part II, the impact of transnational Korean television in America, where Korean television programs very recently pioneered into, is more focused to analyze different trajectories of this emerging media flow in the Western media world. As such, this latter part examines and explores about what makes the transnational flow of Korean television possible and how this emerging flow distinguishes from the constant flow that occurred across the Asia.

Part I

TRANSNATIONAL KOREAN TELEVISION WITH EAST ASIA

Chapter 1

Transforming the Korean Television Industry

The Korean Wave

Asia has changed dramatically since the end of the 1990s, most strikingly in its speedy socioeconomic and cultural transformation, driven by active transnational mobility, diversity, and cultural fluidity across the region. Despite relatively different paces from nation to nation, transnational digital media and technology has increased cultural connectivity, often by boosting national media's regional interpenetration. East Asia occupies the center of this newly developed digital media and technical culture, thanks mainly to the influence of the "Korean Wave." South Korean (hereafter Korean) media content regularly flowed out toward East Asian neighbor countries beginning in 1998–1999 and then extended to Southeast Asia and the Middle East in the early to mid-2000s. Since then, Korean media's overseas distribution had operated on a grander international scale: the Korean Wave or *Hallyu*, as it was coined in the Chinese press, has brought Korean media content into North and South America, as well as Europe.

Both scholars and media industry practitioners have suggested that the Korean Wave is a symbolic phenomenon that unfolds the mixed global cultural dimensions embedded in the transnational and/or transcultural mobility of media, culture, audience, and technology. Based on that definition, this book develops three main points regarding the Korean Wave. First, the Korean Wave represents a rare and innovative media and pop culture flow based off a non-Western media industry, especially in terms of its geographical scope, different media forms, and industrial mechanisms. Second, deeply understanding this cultural diffusion of national media forms requires going beyond a single theory or associated factor. Last but not least, transnational Korean media continues to reach further and broader geographies at different paces and scales, engaging with diversified transnational audience members. Korean television content, including dramas and entertainment shows, notably facilitates this level of transnational mobility for Korean popular culture.

In America, recent media and communication scholarship has produced little research on Asian media and pop culture. In fact, a set of transnational media studies have even been considered farfetched from both American and European perspectives. The limited work on Asian media and pop culture in the U.S. context has examined the macro structure of Asia's regional television and film market, focusing more on its industrial and economic mechanisms and on the global media market order. It often describes a minimal influence of Asian media on global and transnational media industries as well as their intercultural relationships (e.g., Bileby and Harrington 2008; French and Richards 2000; Haven 2006; Moran and Keane 2004; Thussu 2007).

Meanwhile, some Asian researchers have presented an intra- or inter-Asian framework to account for Asian media's transnational movement since the early 2000s, showcasing the production, distribution, and consumption of several Asian TV shows and films (e.g., Cho 2011; Chua 2004; Chua and Iwabuchi 2008; Iwabuchi 2009; Lie 2012). Their models feature keen analyses of increasing transnational flows initiated by a couple of Asian countries and consider how different national media practices influence cultural connectivity within the region. The ubiquitous flow of Korean television shows throughout Asia figures prominently. In Asian contexts, a notable inter-Asian media flow frame identified cultural proximity as the central factor of the Korean Wave, at least at first (Chua 2004; Lee and Ju 2010; Shim 2006; Yang 2008).

Scholars using the cultural proximity theory argued that Asian TV programs present similar sociocultural images and stories enabling other Asians to relate to them better compared to media from the United States or other Western countries. Although most Asian countries have distinct languages, their collective cultural traditions, histories, identities, and modern values are much more similar to each other than to those of Western countries. As a result, Asian television viewers who enjoyed Korean TV programs shared a high level of cultural affinity, finding it easy to connect their real-life personal and social experiences with the portrayed media narratives. Accordingly, previous studies singled out cultural proximity as the reason for Korean television's success across Asia and emphasized the importance of perceived geo-cultural similarity among regional audiences when consuming foreign television programs. Indeed, media content travels well within the same cultural bloc, but not when crossing culturally distant geographical territories.

However, Koichi Iwabuchi refuted the simplicity of the cultural proximity theory to conceive asymmetric inter-Asian media flows, by demonstrating the regional influence of Japanese television and film in many parts of East and Southeast Asia before the Korean Wave. He focused on how the popular TV programs from Japan flowed to different Asian local media and local broadcasts during the 1990s (Iwabuchi 2005). Iwabuchi criticized a core argument of cultural proximity that television viewers neither naturally perceive the similarity of other cultures nor instantly grasp the same cultural elements while they consume other Asian nations' TV programs (Iwabuchi 2008). Instead, he found that television audiences consumed cultural products from other cultures primarily for entertainment, not to identify with specific cultural and audiovisual traits. Moreover, Iwabuchi (2008) made it clear that Asia includes both intra-regional differences and shared similarities, featuring individual national communities rooted in different histories as well as regional power dynamics, which usually work unevenly through politics, economics, and modern social systems. Therefore, though cultural proximity is limited in scope, entertainment media content can be part of a nation's representation among other cultural assets.

Another shortcoming of the cultural proximity theory is that it can explain little about how transnational media flows are constantly recreated, redistributed, and diversified in a new local culture among different local audiences. In cultural proximity theory, one nation's media content is considered the embodiment of a national culture produced by the nation, designated as the static and fixed assets of a nation (Schulze 2013). But in reality, the constitution of a national culture makes it possible to mix inherently with another culture without conscious knowledge through crossing borders using different dimensional mobility. Defining culture in these terms helps clarify the substance of transnational media flows overall.

An intra-Asian or inter-Asian media frame needs to delve into theoretical analyses of former and current Asian media flows. As will be detailed later in this chapter, the Korean Wave was sparked by the regionalization of Korean television serials at the end of the 1990s. It was initiated as part of the historical milieu of decolonization, economic development, Asia's modernization, and resurrection of the regional communal sense, all of which function as cultural and ideological responses to the global hegemony of the West perpetuated in Asia (Yin 2005, 208). When the Asian financial crisis in 1997 cut off the established entertainment industry's traditional funding sources, the competition spurred the rise of independent studios and production companies as a new industry model. Accordingly, the industry was keen to follow the state's encouragement to globalize their markets (Russell and Wehrfritz 2004; Yin 2005). Today, diversified Korean media content is consumed outside of Korea—kept alive by multinational audiences.

These transnational media consumers similarly seek seamless access to Korean television and pop music through their national media networks or the Internet. Continued and broadened diffusion of transnational Korean television has been presented as a counter case of international media and pop culture streams, contrasting with the prevalent international diffusion of U.S. or U.K. television (e.g., Thussu 2008; Tunstall 2008). From a domestic point of view, the Korean Wave greatly influenced the transformation of the Korean broadcasting industry, alongside both regionalization and globalization at the beginning of the 2000s. The Korean television and broadcasting system restructured the domestic media's production and distribution capability, as well as its content innovation.

To understand the complex roles of the Korean Wave in Asian media's global transformation and contribution to transnational cultural mobility, this chapter takes a close look at the East Asian television landscape during the 1990s to establish the previous regional media environment and to describe the East Asian media industry before it faced the media's globalizing drive reinforced by neoliberal globalism.

EAST ASIAN MEDIA LANDSCAPES DURING THE 1990s

Many Asian countries have been distant from their closest neighbors when processing cultural exchanges: as Ryoo (2009, 144) stated, "[Asian nations] have had a tendency to link more closely to the former colonial empires or advanced Western countries than with neighbors sharing borders." Until the end of the 1990s, most East Asian countries depended primarily on domestic TV programs for both production and consumption; only a few foreign TV shows, usually produced in the United States or United Kingdom, made the prime time broadcast on East Asian television. Japan did export TV shows and animations to the region for several years, in particular to Taiwan and Hong Kong, but most East Asian TV programs were consumed domestically. The East Asian television industry was neither sizable nor marketable when it came to flowing out across national borders. Indeed, there was no signal of active interregional media flow within East Asia, except for Japan, until the late 1990s. In this vein, the East Asian television industry showed a heavy influence from the center-peripheral media flow in light of the global media system.

Asia's 1997 financial crisis made a big change in the East Asian media industry and the regional television flow, complicating the media landscape within East Asia. The new century rapidly transformed the Asian economy into a part of a neoliberal global system directed by the Western-led global finance system (e.g., the International Monetary Fund). Facing desperate economic downturns, East Asian countries demanded a boost of their national economies beyond locally manufactured assets, so they considered new values in entertainment media and popular culture commodities. Specifically, the Korean government found it hard to overlook the economic impact of U.S.

and other Western television imports into the country. In addition, Japan was its only East Asian neighbor available for television exports, but domestic TV programs occupied more than 95 percent of its entire broadcast schedule (Iwabuchi 2004a). Indeed, Japan was the forerunner of Asian media flows: it had adopted a modern style of TV series in the early 1990s, especially targeting urban young adults beginning their adult lives in big cities (Lee 2004; Yang 2008).

Barker (2002) argued that globalization in the realm of media and popular culture has reinforced a simultaneous dual swing as the result of the ideological conflict between transnational commercialism and the resurrection of nationalism. Thus, on one side, global media firms notably grounded in Western countries (e.g. the U.S.-based media conglomerates) actively launched in Asia's regional media markets, utilizing their dominant market hegemony. On the other side, the rising national media or national production of media system within the region that were formerly less connected, such as the Asian media industry, at least had to revamp their processes against the prowess of global media from the West. In this immersive globalization, East Asia's regional media flow emerged in an increasing pace of intra-regional circulation of its domestic television programs, formats, and production systems. At first, the intra-regional media produced free circulation of a few regional pop culture commodities, which continued to accompany regional media players' investment finances, production cooperation, and copyright ownership more dynamically within East Asia (Moran and Keane 2004).

To explain global media flows in non-Western regions, Thussu (2007) pointed out that international media agents existed in Asia previously, including both private and state-sponsored media firms, and that the Indian film industry fit this level of a global media player until the end of 1990s. In his view, a national support media system took the place of the established TV industry model in East Asia, so this protected broadcast industry under the state or national power was perceived as the mainstream until global media players arose in the region. This led East Asian media industries to rapidly change their systems and market orders, just to survive the active penetration of global media conglomerates toward each nation. Thussu suggested that layering within international media agents granted considerable cultural influences in the region and the world, expressed as geo-cultural media caterers who possessed large media shares in a certain regional culture bloc. He identified the recent role of the Korean media industry across Asian regional media markets as one such caterer. Accordingly, Thussu stressed that the layered international media players from local, regional, and global media agents became more organized nationally or regionally supported media industry. In part, East Asian countries' media, in Japan, Hong Kong, and most recently Korea, excel at this regional media interplay:

State-supported initiatives have also been an important contributing factor for the globalization of cultural products. In South Korea, for example, state policies of a quota system for local films and support for such events as the Pusan International Film Festival, have put Korean cinema on the world map. (Thussu 2007, 14)

Along similar lines, the media export data for the international flow shows a certain pattern: cultural factors and taste differences among transnational audiences vary the preference of the exported media content from foreign media industries—indeed, domestic TV programs are always the first preference for each foreign audience to choose. Tunstall (2008, 245) illuminated this nature of global media flows in exporting content: "Nation-states and regional blocs at the top of the pecking order export to those below them; national and regional blocs at the bottom of the pecking order import from those above them." As indicated, intra- and interregional exchanges of media capital, content, and production crews across East Asia has increased and developed multifaceted local strategies against strong global media conglomerates since the late 1990s. The East Asian media industry and market thus began to reshape its infrastructure, operating mechanisms, and organizational formation. National or state-sponsored media models in East Asia—China, Taiwan, Hong Kong, and Korea—confronted active globalization initiatives (Chan and Ma 1996; French and Richard 2000; Hukill 2000; Ish 1996; Oba and Chan-Olmested 2005), and even the top-tier Japanese media industry was challenged by other growing regional media players.

In analyzing the Japanese media distribution to Asia, Yoshino (1999) pinpointed that nationalism in Asia reinstated a rising sense of national consciousness, cultivated national identity, and stressed domestic culture and history, all of which were simultaneously growing under globalization. The resurrection of nationalism within Asia in this early global age appeared to be a dual phenomenon, combining the formal, nation-sponsored process with the informal, market-oriented process. For example, Japanese media and popular culture have pursued a sophisticated blend of contrasting tastes between the West and East in their popular entertainment content. Japanese TV shows, animated films, and manga (Japanese comic books) have attracted more foreign viewers in the West than the East in terms of market share. In general, the Japanese media industry, using a nation-sponsored model, has established foreign target markets with a dual strategy: obtain standardized market appeals first and then represent sensitivity to the regional market (Yoshino 1999).

Given this conflict of globalization throughout Asia, at first the Japanese media industry experienced not only an increase of intra-regional media flow but also a backlash against their own media exports among

Asian audiences, due to resurrected nationalism in each nation. A set of Japanese animations, television dramas, and variety shows traveled well to East and Southeast Asian regions before the late 1990s—scholars and critics referred to this as the Japanese Wave (Moran and Keane 2004)—but the peak of Japanese television exports waned later in the 1990s. Koichi Iwabuchi (2002, 24–35) characterized the 1990s move of Japanese media into Asia as the success of culturally "odorless" media consumption by regional audiences. Japanese animations, television programs, and video games at the time contained intentionally little sense of Japan-ness and did not foreground authentic Japanese identities in narrative and audiovisual elements. This culturally neutral-flavored media form spurred Japanese TV dramas and anime to be exported across Asian regions, compared to Western media markets.

The Korean Wave has often been discussed in similar terms: as a regional media flow model based on a national-sponsored media, following the earlier Japanese media flow. Although these two transnational media flows have superficial commonalities, they feature different content forms and flow mechanisms (Lee 2004). The major difference between these consecutive media flows within Asia is the genre difference in drawing regional audiences. While Japanese pop music, fashion magazines, comics (e.g., manga), and animations were the most popular content of the Japanese Wave, the Korean Wave has spread through popular mass media content such as TV drama series, pop music, and films. Another difference is that the Japanese Wave originated from an emerging politics of *Asianism* in Japan, so the flow was planned as a way of rebuilding regional relationships to replace the historical image of Japan as a non-Western colonizer against Asia (Iwabuchi 2008; Yoshino 1999). However, the Korean Wave likely happened more by chance at the end of 1990s, in response to Asia's global initiative moment. As the Korean Wave has sustained itself in the region, it has made reciprocal media exchanges to integrate the East Asian media through coproduction, partnership, and remake opportunities.

Overall, the current circuit of transnational Korean media, including the Korean Wave, positively contributes to improving the quality of the nation's audiovisual media industry. The Korean Wave has led to a rapid transformation of the nation's television systems, TV production mechanisms, and culture industry. In turn, the Korean Wave represents a very critical moment in Korea's pro-market shift toward neoliberal globalization, as the Korean broadcasting industry anticipates the rise of their home-produced television programs overseas. The Korean broadcasting industry has forged new paths to overcome both the narrow and competitive domestic media outlets in various ways, such as stable financing, selective programming, promotional planning, and international distribution systems.

THE KOREAN WAVE AND KOREAN TV DRAMA

While scholars and industry experts define *Korean Wave* in slightly different ways, overall it describes the increasing transnational distribution and consumption of various Korean media genres and pop culture products, including TV programs, pop music, films, online games, fashion artifacts, and smartphones (Jeong 2012; Jin 2016; Ju 2017; Kim 2013; Lie 2012; Madrid-Morales and Lovric 2015; Ryoo 2009; Shim 2006; Sung 2013). In February 2016, BBC Radio aired a seventy-two-minute feature show entitled *South Korea: The Silent Cultural Superpower*. Its trailer featured this line: "From movies and TV to K-Pop, South Korean culture manages to punch far above its weight across East Asia, and beyond. But how did this happen, and why is it so important to Koreans?" (BBC Radio 3, 2016). Likewise, Korean television and pop culture eventually caught the attention of non-Asian media producers and marketers, including well-known Western media players in the United States and United Kingdom. For a long time, the Korean media industry has been marginalized in terms of both global media and transnational audiences due to its size and less standard marketability. While the Korean Wave hit the Asian media market, only few anticipated the growth of Korean television, movies, and music on different continents.

Over the past two decades, the Korean Wave has evolved new diffusion and consumption processes overseas, distinguishing it from earlier phases of the Korean Wave. Indeed, scholars often refer to the early stage as "Hallyu 1.0," especially focusing on Korean TV dramas' phenomenal popularity across Asia (Jeong et al. 2017; Jin 2016; Kim 2015). Korean TV dramas were the first mainstream content to flow out and achieve regional popularity, but since the late 2000s—the "Hallyu 2.0" stage—Korean popular music (K-pop) performed by idol bands has quickly replaced K-dramas' hype (Hong-Mercier 2013; Jin 2016; Kim 2015; Lie 2012). K-pop attracts even broader transnational audiences, streaming into the Middle East, North and South America, and Europe. It is not unusual for K-pop fans from different continents to enjoy typical Korean-style pop music.[1] In accordance with the global K-pop boom, Hallyu 2.0 brings more attention to its cultural roles and diverse impacts on the deepened transnational Korean media flows and consumption environments, led by the Internet and social media.

In short, the breakpoint of the Korean Wave happened shortly after the Asian financial crisis between 1997 and 1998, during which Korea liberalized its own market under the pressure of globalization, mainly from the U.S. government. This triggered a radical transformation of the Korean television industry as a whole (Ju 2014). Both financial and economic factors since the early 1990s have instigated the growth of the entertainment industry and film industries as the part of the nation's new economic vision, and Korean business conglomerates were able to invest funding in different types of media corporations, thanks to new legislation. Korea's national interest in its entertainment industry was broadened because of economic factors—such as the burgeoning middle classes, increased economic development, and a continuing vision of economic growth—which fueled the demand to expand the media and culture industry.

From 1998 to the mid-2000s, the Korean government turned its attention to developing innovative economic resources that focused more on the culture and information-based economy, rather than on the conventional manufacturing economy. As the leading initiative, television stations, broadcasting associations, telecommunication companies, and government ministries in Korea created proactive audiovisual content industries, so home-produced media content could effectively capitalize on both domestic and overseas markets (Ju 2014). Since the early 2000s, the Korean media industry has rapidly changed from a nation-protected to one featuring free-market competition driven by private ownership. This made multichannel broadcasting possible, as well as commercial initiatives sponsored by the private broadcasting system, which was profoundly affected by commercialism and deregulation (Shim and Jin 2007). The situation was similar to other East Asian nations to a certain extent: the broader East Asian media industry simultaneously began a structural transformation, adding a myriad of cable and satellite channels in each nation's television systems (Ju 2014).

However, it is important to note that the birth of the Korean Wave centered on the Chinese television market, not on a planned initiative by Korean broadcasters or the Korean government itself. The Chinese attraction to Korean TV dramas was a result of a timely matrix of factors, including the multilayered, transnational mobility of people, information, and cultural capital across many East and South Asian countries (Hong-Mercier 2013; Kim 2015). Korean TV dramas have proven especially compelling to other Asian viewers, and John Lie (2012) reinforced that the Korean Wave in its initial articulation seemed to be all about Korean soap operas. Similarly, Shim (2008) accounted for the rising popularity and improved production quality of Korean TV dramas based on increasing competition of the domestic media combined with the favorable Asian television market. The Korean broadcasting industry later focused more actively on capitalizing their media products abroad, as the three major TV networks in Korea undertook a vital restructuring of their broadcast systems in the hopes of growing their regional media production and distribution (Ju 2017).

In the primary reform, the Korean television industry adapted the logic of neoliberal capitalism driven by growing market competition and a nation-supported commercial drive. This took advantage of the demand for Korean media content by regional Asia and actually created a new outlet for Korea's domestic media content. The Korean Wave, in this sense, came at an opportune moment when East Asian television industries had a high demand for Korean television to feed their increasing cable and satellite channels. The Korean broadcasting industry responded rapidly to proactive regional media markets, along with producing homegrown television dramas. National support of the Korean broadcasting industry also took advantage of its cultural or political diplomacy to broaden the Korean Wave. For example, to complement the cohosting of the World Cup in 2002, TBS Entertainment (Japan) and MBC Production (Korea) collaborated for the first time in the two countries' media history to coproduce a TV drama, *Friends*. This sixty-minute, two-episode series featured a romance between a Japanese woman and a Korean man, who overcome the prejudices and doubts of friends and family to become a sincere international couple. It was intended to convey the new friendship between Korea and Japan in the twenty-first century, leaving the two countries' bitter history behind. Following this, Korea's national broadcaster Korean Broadcasting System (KBS) and China Central Television (CCTV) collaborated on another TV drama, *My Love Beijing*, to mark the tenth anniversary of diplomatic relations between the two countries (Yin 2005).

KOREAN TELEVISION PROGRAM EXPORTS

The Korean Wave has increased the volume of Korean television program exports for the past two decades. Although the export figures alone should not determine how we comprehend the Korean Wave, they do provide tangible information to review the scale and market shares of Korean TV programs overseas.

As figure 1.1 shows, between 2003 and 2015, the total revenue of Korean TV exports increased by nearly eight times, from $27 million to $216 million. Broadcasters' total export revenues surpassed the total imports of foreign programs—mainly imported from the United States and Japan—in 2005, when the export revenue of $106 million more than doubled the import revenue of $43 million. The export volume was relatively low between 2007 and 2008, however, when several East Asian countries enacted import restriction policies in an attempt to resist the Korean Wave (Ahn 2014; Ryoo 2009). This reduced the revenues of both years, with the lowest at slightly more than $93 million. Export revenues, however, rebounded in 2009, and, in 2010, the export revenue reached $127 million. By 2014 the total export revenue by Korean broadcasters was $256 million—the highest export revenue of the period, approximately a tenfold increase from the 2003 revenue of $27 million.

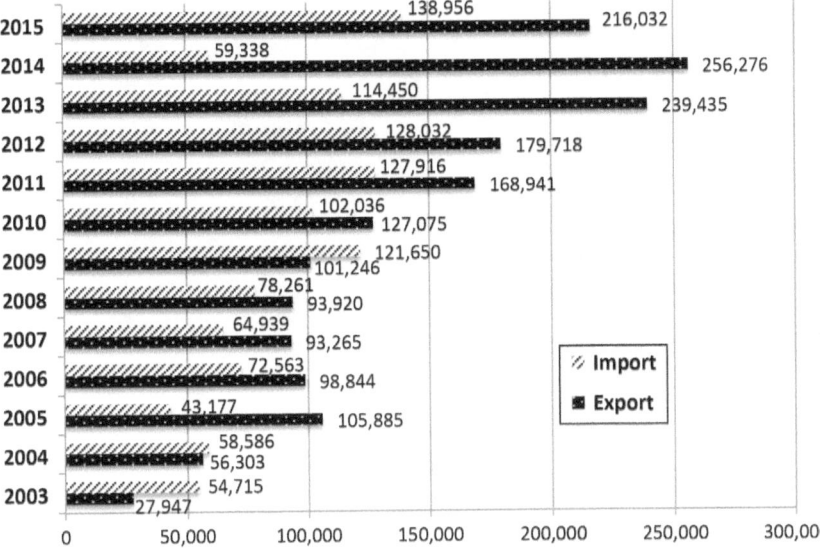

Figure 1.1 **Korean TV Program Exports by Annual Revenues.** *Note:* The unit of revenue is U.S. $1000. *Source:* Author's creation of the chart using the published statistical data. Broadcasting Industry White Paper (2004–2006) by Korea Communication Commission; Broadcasting Industry White Paper (2010–2011) by the Ministry of Culture, Sports, and Tourism (MCST); Broadcasting Industry White Paper (2012) and Content Industry Statistics (2014–2015) by Korea Creative Content Agency (KOCCA); Broadcasting Industry Report (2013, 2016) by the Ministry of Science, ICT and Future Planning (MSIF).

Among television program exports, TV dramas have consistently occupied the largest share versus other TV genres, growing from 76.8 percent in 2002 to 96.2 percent in 2005, followed by documentary and entertainment (see figure 1.2). The tendency continued until 2012, when dramas' share of TV exports dropped from 94.9 percent (in 2011) to about 85 percent (Ju 2017). This downturn continued through 2015, when drama exports only reached 79.6 percent, but dramas still held a decisive advantage over other genres, such as variety and entertainment (14.4%) and sports (2.4%) (Ministry of Science, ICT and Future Planning 2016).

As the Korean Wave has advanced, Korean TV drama also gained transnational popularity and especially diversified its generic impact, unlike other countries' drama series. For instance, a 2014 study of Chinese youth's Korean TV consumption showed that Korean drama was still the most preferred genre to consume at 69.4 percent, followed by entertainment shows (67.1%) and K-pop (63%), regardless of age differences among the sampled youths (Ahn 2014). The importance of Korean TV dramas in the export of Korean television is clear in the export data. In response, as I discuss more in

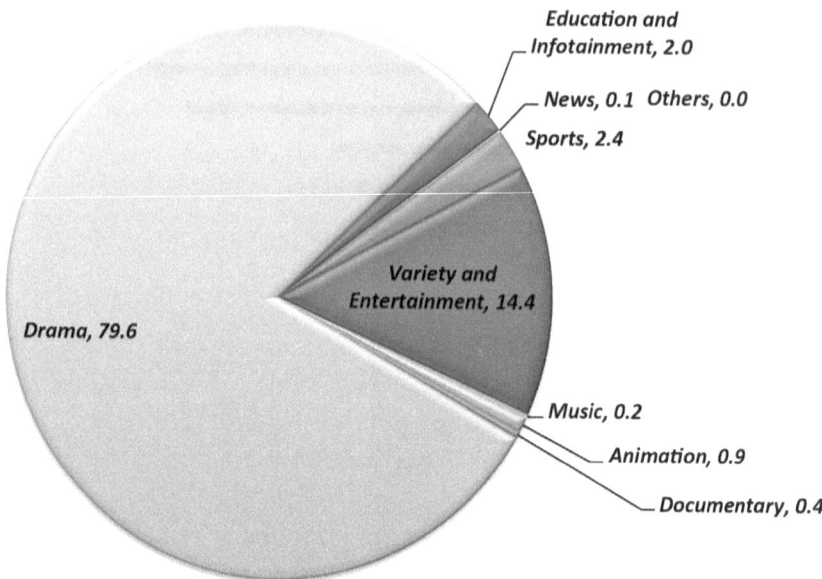

Figure 1.2 Korean TV Program Exports by Genre (2015). *Note*: The unit of figure is percent (%). *Source*: Author's creation of the chart using the published statistical data; Broadcasting Industry Report (2016) by the Ministry of Science, ICT and Future Planning (MSIF).

chapters 2 and 3, the Korean television industry has created different marketing and promotional tactics to extend its commercial value and distribution cycles.

In tandem with the transnational success of Korean TV drama, the Western media (mainly U.S. and U.K. journalists) account for the Korean Wave as a reflective cultural incident that created growth in regional cultural dynamics across East Asia by leading the region's entangled politics, economy, and cultural hegemony. Due to the emotional sensitivity originating from East Asian historical ties, the Korean Wave actually provoked a historical sensibility of nostalgia among people in China, Japan, and Korea. Japan's colonial occupation of other East Asian countries in the early 1900s has remained a subject of tension within the region. Fears and antagonism have been directed toward the former colonizer, especially since Japan has spread its media and pop culture to the region. For instance, China and Korea legislatively restricted the importation of Japanese content into their media markets until the late 1990s. Korea, in fact, was the last country to open its cultural market to Japanese media and pop culture in 1998.

Japan's negative historical legacy in East Asia and other parts of Asia has tended to be a barrier, resulting in Japan paying a higher price for cultural discounts—a concept suggested by Hoskins and Mirus (1988) pertinent to media exports.[2] By comparison, Korean TV dramas were more readily accepted in the Asian media market without the cultural barriers that the Japanese media had: Korean media content seems to be more culturally or emotionally welcomed by Asian audiences than Japanese media content. It seems many Chinese viewers share the similar point of view to Norimitsu Onish, who said in a 2006 interview, "There is no obstacle to our accepting South Korean culture, unlike Japanese culture" (New York Times, 2006).

Moreover, a report on National Public Radio in the United States suggested that Korean television drama depicts a shared sense of Asian culture: "Those are Confucian values like the importance of family, obedience and respect for one's elders. Values that many Chinese feel they've lost" (Lim 2006). In the author's analysis, sustained Confucian morals and values are well embodied in Korean dramas' plots and narratives, and more interestingly, Korean dramas advance the image of modern Asia as well as its unique lifestyles as the object of yearning for many Asian people. Indeed, lucrative urban lifestyles and sophisticated capitalist ideology are highly visible in transnational Korean dramas, showing mediated westernized modernity as a common value in many parts of modernizing Asia. The Western model of capitalism sets up a primary standard of life and drives Asian people to pursue similar concepts of happiness and success in their own individual and social lives. What they have been seen from the Western media is also meant for their own life standards, despite the represented cultural difference. Interestingly, Korean TV drama plays a significant role in filtering unfavorable values contained in Western television programs, by appropriately mingling Korea's traditional thoughts about Confucian morals with the dominant modern images in many Asian countries (Chua 2004; Lin and Tong 2008). Korean television producers and production crews are very skillful in their sophisticated portrayals of contemporary Asians' genuine lives, applying emotional sensitivity and stylish audiovisual techniques (Chua 2004; Hanaki et al. 2007).

In 2015, the majority of Korean TV programs were still consumed in Asia (91.3%); Japan consumed the largest share at 33 percent, followed by China (24.3%), Taiwan (10.1%), Hong Kong (5.1%), Thai (4.5%), and Vietnam (4.2%). While Korean program exports dropped in Japan by more than 50 percent in previous years (2010–2012), Chinese imports of Korean TV programs have continued to rise, such that China is expected to soon be the largest importer of Korean television. Outside of Asia, Korean programs continued to improve their export share in the United States (6.8%), France (0.2%), and the United Kingdom (0.1%). In terms of geographical distribution, Korean TV programs flowed into North America (7.0%), South America (0.2%), and Europe (1.2%). Specifically, Korean TV programs exported to the United States were valued at $14 million in 2015, an increase of 25 percent from 2013 ($9.3 million), and America became the largest non-Asian importer of Korean TV programs (Ministry of Science, ICT and Future Planning 2016). As noted, Korean program exports to Europe and South America represented the lower ratio; hence, South America and Eastern Europe have become new cultural markets for Korean television, as the Korean Wave only arrived there in 2012.

Harrington and Bielby (2005) stressed that the success of media products in international marketplaces relates to the brand identity of local or national media commodities. To TV program buyers in an international trade fair, a solid brand identity for a certain media product enhances the reputation of local or national media's content value, which indicates the program's potential quality, universal popularity, or longevity. Therefore, the constructed brand identity of a national media is commonly generated from specific TV genres and the form of a national media product. For instance, Brazil has a TV brand for its telenovelas, Scandinavian countries for reality shows, and Japan for its animations (Harrington and Bielby 2005). Before the Korean Wave, Korea had neither a brand identity nor a reputation of programming quality as a national TV producer, so the lack of reputation of Korean TV content was a huge cultural discount when conducting international trades (Ju 2017). Regardless, Korean TV drama became a gateway to broader interest in Korean pop culture or the Korean Wave in the global media market, and it continues to reach far-flung cultural markets.

THE KOREAN TELEVISION SYSTEM AND BROADCASTING CORPORATIONS

It is helpful to understand the Korean television system and broadcasting mechanisms to analyze the Korean Wave, so this section presents a brief typology of the current television industry in Korea. In the Korean television system, three network TV stations (KBS, MBC, and SBS) and independent production companies are the primary television program producers. For domestic TV programming, network broadcasters have dominated all genres of TV programs, thanks to their self-feeding channels and scheduling authority, and the three networks have held strong hegemony in the Korean television longer than the recently booming cables and other independent TV production studios. The first significant turning point in Korean TV drama production occurred in the late 1990s, with multichannel broadcasting via satellite and extended cable services. Due to the availability of more TV channels, the higher demand for TV dramas in Korean television timetable led to a significant surge in producing dramas; therefore, this genre became the most precious business entity in the Korean television industry (Ju 2017).

Starting in the mid-2000s, independent production studios in Korea rapidly grew and expanded the size and scope of their production capability. A couple of independent production companies, however, appeared to be primarily TV drama production houses, having a coproduction system with the three networks. The so-called top five production companies were born at the time: Olive9, KJH Production, PAN Entertainment, SamHwa Production, and Chorokbaem Media. These large independent production studios began with former network TV producers, directors, screenwriters, entertainment agents, and cinematographers, and they often merged with talent agencies. An increase in domestic competition and advertising-based profit making models caused an inevitable rise in the average production cost per Korean drama; as one solution, joint ventures appeared to provide an alternative funding method for both networks and independent production studios. Since then, the Korean television industry has turned into a dual production system between networks and independent production studios, particularly when producing Korean drama (Ju 2017; Park 2013).

During the Hallyu 1.0 era (1998–2008), network TV stations built a heavy star marketing strategy for their own drama series to increase their impact overseas. For example, the great success of *DaeJangGeum*[3] (MBC, 2003) for domestic viewers strongly supported an export of this drama to more than eighty countries across Asia, the Middle East, South and North America, and Europe. Promotion of newly released (or soon-to-be-released) Korean dramas at the time activated in foreign local markets, along with preplanned promotion events from city to city, were a popular marketing form. Meanwhile, the stars in the popular Korean dramas contributed profiles of featured cast members, behind-the-scenes stories, guidebooks, and local fan meetings. Thus, the so-called K-drama celebrities were born and they became the most valuable asset for pursuing large exports of each drama all around Asia. For example, dramas such as *TaeWangSaSinGi* (MBC), *Coffee Prince* (MBC), *Sorry and Love You* (SBS), and *IRIS* (KBS) were preferred by Asian TV buyers because their leads were top-tier K-drama stars well-known among pan-Asian audiences: Bae Yong-Joon in *TaeWangSaSinGi*, Gong Yu in *Coffee Prince*, So Ji-Sub in *Sorry and Love You*, and Lee Byung-Hun in *IRIS* (Ju 2014).

Riding the Korean Wave, KBS, a state TV network, restructured its international sales unit in 2000 to focus on selling produced dramas outside of Korea instead of importing foreign programs into the country. The new unit belonged separately to KBS Media, the subsidiary company, which managed all sales of KBS copyrighted shows to both domestic and foreign markets, actively involving the state-run networks in its international trade. In addition, KBS took advantage of the nation's diplomatic policy to develop cooperative business relationships with foreign public or state televisions, such as NHK in Japan, CCTV in China, and the BBC in the UK. As a result, they were able to use these partnerships to establish new contracts with foreign TV studios. For example, one of the popular Korean dramas *Winter Sonata* began with NHK's terrestrial broadcast in 2003–2004 and marked a megahit on viewers' ratings as of the foreign TV series in Japan's TV broadcast. According to a personal interview with KBS Media sales managers in 2008, the former NHK-KBS coproduction relationship for a documentary program specified the sale of the exclusive rights for *Winter Sonata* to be broadcast on NHK, which is a state-run network in Japan (Ju 2017).

Most recently, KBS, MBC, and SBS have faced heavier competition for domestic TV market share in Korea. These networks' terrestrial broadcast powers have been challenged by the emerging high-profile cable networks such as TVN and OCN and by newly deregulated broadcasters called comprehensive TV channels[4], including JTBC. More and more, these growing new broadcasters can afford to produce their original drama series and air them on subscription TV platforms outside of the traditional network TV system (Ju 2017). Not surprisingly, OCN, JTBC, and TVN's dramas in particular have recently become more appealing to the domestic audience. Dramas produced by TVN such as *Signal* (2016), along with the *Reply 1997* (2012), *Reply 1994* (2014), and *Reply 1988* (2016) series, broke records for the all-time cable TV drama ratings, and brought TVN onto the stage as a new K-drama production house, compelling enhancements in K-drama production by three network stations.

Nowadays, Korean network broadcasters often face strong competition for obtaining high audience shares against both TVN and JTBC when they simulcast their new drama series. This is somewhat similar to U.S. television, where new Netflix original series can get more attention than ABC's or NBC's new seasons or pilot series. TVN in particular has rapidly grown its competitive programming capability during the past ten years within the Korean domestic TV market, becoming a primary sector for Korean drama production by significantly increasing viewership of its original dramas as well as entertainment shows. TVN has differentiated its drama programming via subgenre series (e.g., crime and detective series, fantasy romance, and comedy) to divide the market share of the overall Korean dramas that had long been dominated by the three main networks. In 2017, Netflix, the global content streaming company based in the United States, announced active partnerships and licensing agreements with Korean content production houses, as well as with third-party production companies, to deliver more Korean television programs and films through their global platforms to over 190 countries worldwide (Sohn 2018). Along with this plan, Netflix and JTBC signed an exclusive broadcast license deal to broadcast 600 hours of JTBC's original dramas and variety shows on Netflix's global streaming platform. TVN has also had a couple of drama series streamed on Netflix recently (*Misaeng: Incomplete*

Life, Signal, and *Stranger*) because of a 2016 content partnership agreement between Netflix and CJ E&M, which is the parent company of TVN. In April 2017, TVN's drama *Man To Man* was streamed on Netflix for the first, subtitled in twenty different languages (Netflix 2017), and very recently in 2018 *Mr. Sunshine*, a new TVN's original drama, exclusively streamed on Netflix for the overseas viewers at the exactly same broadcast schedule from TVN in Korea (a two-episode broadcast every weekend). In addition, Studio Dragon, an independent drama production firm that is a subsidy of TVN but independent from CJ E&M, has continued a special streaming license with Netflix regarding some of their original series over the years, in consideration of the partnership between Netflix and CJ E&M (Netflix 2017; Sohn 2018).

Entering the age of convergence between television and the Internet, all the Korean networks quickly adopted format trade and international sales of K-drama broadcast rights that also include video streaming licenses overseas. This not only expands the life cycle of Korean TV programs, but also broadens their accessibility to international audiences. As the forerunner in this trend, MBC made a deal to send its dramas to DramaFever, a multilingual video streaming service in the United States, in a 2001 agreement allowing a short turnaround or even a simultaneous schedule with the drama's first domestic run. SBS followed suit shortly; its dramas have been distributed to Internet viewers from around the world via DramaFever and other streaming licenses, including Hulu and Netflix (Ju 2017). In 2016, when KBS broadcast its original drama *Descendants of the Sun* via the KBS-2 channel in Korea, the drama was simultaneously streamed on the two Chinese streaming sites, IQiyi and YouKu, a consequence of a Chinese media group's investment in the drama production. Both the Korean TV ratings and the Chinese online streaming hits were tremendous, and the drama sold its broadcast rights to twenty-seven countries while it was first airing in Korea (Song 2016). No doubt, the drama was soon up and running through Netflix for the U.S. viewers.

Above all, the Korean Wave has facilitated an outward orientation for the Korean television industry, allowing it to join the global media industry with a new form of television programming. Moreover, it has challenged the Korean television system to respond efficiently to the plethora of new media technologies, coupled with different cultural products embedding a new sensibility from the East to the West.

NOTES

1. Korean idol music is classified as a performer-based dance music style contrasting with conventional Western pop music genres such as hip-hop, rock, and R&B, which are composed of versatile styles of musical rhythms and beats. However,

K-pop is likely to be understood in terms of the idol music that often melds Korean and Western pop music genres. Furthermore, K-pop singers' exotic group dance choreographies have become an emblem of K-pop. These Korean idol singers are usually all-around entertainers who are primarily trained, created, and managed by the unique Korean entertainment agent system.

2. The cultural discount model explains that media programs rooted in one nation (or culture) have diminished appeal for audiences elsewhere. In international media trade, cultural discounts are an important factor when evaluating the purchase of a certain TV show or film for audiences or consumers in other geo-cultural territories. Overall, foreign media content increases the chance that viewers find it more difficult to identify storylines and textual meanings (compared to domestic content) because foreign content is produced with different languages, styles, values, and beliefs based on different cultural or national senses. Often, these factors hinder foreign audiences from easily receiving and relating to specific programs from abroad (Ang 1985; Iwabuchi 2004, 2005; Lee 2004; Morley 2006). If a TV program is produced in a different language from its original production, the program tends to appeal less to local audiences in different countries compared to the original program.

3. *DaeJangGeum* is a fifty-four-episode historical drama series produced by MBC (a terrestrial network of Korea) in 2003. *Jewel in the Palace* is competitively used as the English title. This historical drama first broadcast in Korea and gained huge popularity among domestic audiences, then the drama's broadcast rights were sold to over 120 countries across Asia, the Americas, and Europe. Shortly after the initial broadcast of *DaeJangGeum* in Korea, its international popularity was broadly proclaimed, and it has been considered one of the best Korean TV dramas among many transnational audiences. For example, the drama was selected in 2005 as the most-watched TV shows of the year in Hong Kong (Kim 2013). *DaeJangGeum* featured a dramatic period story about the first female royal physician *Jang Geum* (female leader) in the later Joseon Dynasty (1600s–1700s) in Korea. She was an orphan who grew up in the royal Joseon palace as one of the kitchen servants. She became a top chef to the king and later the first female royal physician, overcoming many risks, hurdles, and difficulties due to her female gender and low class identity.

4. Comprehensive TV channels in the Korean television industry can be understood as paid-TV channels offering subscriptions via multiple media platforms, such as cable, IPTV, and satellite (KT Skylife). These channels can produce and broadcast their original TV programs of various genres, such as news, variety, documentary, sports, and drama series. Comprehensive TV channels operate by airing their programs for subscribers only, depending on the selected platform, under contractual agreements with subscribers (Ministry of Culture, Sports, and Tourism 2012). In December 2011, four comprehensive TV channels in Korea started their first broadcast certified by the Korea Communication Commission: JTBC, MBN, TV Chosun, and Channel A.

Chapter 2

Korean TV Drama Narratives

Are Korean Dramas a Transcultural Story?

In the previous chapter, I provided an overview of transnational flows of Korean television programs and outlined the birth and rise of the Korean Wave. In the context of the transformation of the Korean television industry, driven by media globalization in terms of both institutional and industrial perspectives, I emphasized the value of Korean TV dramas (K-dramas hereafter) in the ongoing Korean Wave as a transnational media flow of non-Western cultural origin. This framework helps explain why the Korean Wave occurred and how it was sustained for more than a decade. Certainly, K-dramas have been the chief promoter of the Korean Wave beyond geo-cultural territorialities. More recently, during the Hallyu 2.0 phase, K-dramas have been constantly disseminated and loved among broader transnational audiences outside of Asia, as documented by several studies on Korean media consumption (see Correra 2012; Hong-Mercier 2013; Han 2017; Hübinette 2012; Ju and Lee 2015; Kim 2013; Jeong et al. 2017; Jung 2009; Lee et al. 2014; Oh 2014; Oh 2015; Otmazgin and Lyan 2013; Yang 2008; Yang 2012).

In this chapter, I turn my attention to K-drama fans and transnational audiences, especially in terms of how K-dramas provoke the reconstruction of a certain semantic structure while consuming and entertaining viewers with common narrative themes, plots, audiovisual images, and manifested cultural symbols. So far, media scholarship in the United States has largely ignored what attracts and motivates Western viewers of TV programs that originate from Asia, or how and why K-dramas (or even Korean TV programs more broadly) are accepted or not by U.S. viewers. To fill this gap, this chapter delves into the overall values, meanings, and roles of K-dramas for different transnational audiences, presenting the K-drama as a specific media form that enables viewers to construct different levels of engagement, participation, and identification.

As we all know, broadcasters and online TV providers generally decide which programs to produce, but individual viewers choose whether to watch a particular program. Hence, it is important to know how and why K-dramas' narratives and modes of storytelling appeal to transnational and/or transcultural audiences, especially when other foreign TV choices are available. K-dramas' storytelling, I argue, enables transnational TV viewers to experience a different source of pleasure with regard to decoding each drama's narratives and symbolic elements. In turn, this experience helps them decide whether or not they want to relate to K-dramas.

Media scholars and TV program providers have recognized that the soap opera is one TV genre that transports well across borders (Bielby and Harrington 2008; Haven 2006). TV soap operas from America and the UK, and particularly telenovelas—daily soap opera series produced by many Latin American TV studios—prove the international competitive marketability of this genre. TV soap operas feature the serialization of a story over an extended period of time that illustrates emotional themes, as they peer into people's relationships and everyday lives. While telenovela series do have central storylines focusing on family, romantic relationships, emotions, and conflicts, these are apparently universal themes despite a strong manifestation of Latin culture. The international popularity of soap operas on television not only testifies to the genre's ability to explore specific properties associated with cultural sentiment in narratives, but also its capacity to vary those narratives with pluralistic, local symbolic narratives at the same time. This allows the easy translatability of many different soap operas, of multinational origins, in transnational contexts.

In tandem with the universal narrative of serial TV dramas, Jason Mittell advanced an interesting argument that might be more appropriate to understanding narrative complexity in different TV serials, by defining the storytelling mode of TV serials separately from other typified fictional TV genre categories, such as comedies and dramas. In his view, popular TV serials enact a universal narrative theme as well as certain structural elements, regardless of whether the series is typically categorized as a detective or crime series, fantasy, daily soap opera, or adventure. Across all TV genres, universal narratives of television fiction are notably recognized as romance or melodrama narratives.

Using this model, Mittell (2015, 244) characterized the essence of melodrama as a storytelling mode that uses certain ways to evoke emotional revelation with regards to love relationships. "This more expansive definition of melodrama as mode rather than genre," he noted, "unites various forms of serial television via a shared commitment to linking morality, emotional response, and narrative drive." Considering American and British TV serials, Mittell (2015) articulated that popular television series crossing national borders have adopted complex narratives as an identified storytelling mode. For example, *Alias*, *Sherlock*, *24*, and *Lost* are famous Anglophone TV series that created passionate fan bases beyond their production origins, and all these series establish complicated plot puzzles in their main narrative structures across many TV seasons. In comparison, the popular K-dramas have been classified internationally as types of soap opera or melodrama series by many Western media critics and scholars, because K-dramas often portray romance or romance-forefront narratives.

By and large, K-dramas' narrative composition exhibits quintessential differences from their counterparts in the United States, the United Kingdom, or Latin America in terms of storytelling modes and of textual and visual structures. Mittell's notion of a storytelling mode is well-suited to analyze culturally nuanced TV drama series, to produce a multilayered examination of K-dramas' appeals to transnational audiences even though their narrative arcs rely heavily on Korea's domestic and cultural contexts and embedded ideological sensibilities. Put simply, the storytelling mode of a Korean TV drama referring to Mittell's approach is to explore the substance of Korean dramas' pleasures in narrative arcs and thematic appeals that specially connect to the heart of transnational audiences for that drama.

In this chapter, I examine the substance of the most common romance narratives in Korean dramas, showcasing a storytelling mode that uncovers the unique appeal of K-dramas consumed by transnational audiences. For a qualitative and critical analysis on K-dramas' narratives and textual forms in accordance with the actual viewer's involvement, I adopt different data sets that include the author's personal interviews with Asian American K-drama viewers (2011), review comments for Korean TV show on the U.S. Netflix (2016–2018), and both newspapers and broadcast interviews regarding K-dramas. This mixed data and qualitative analysis investigate the translatability of the Korean romance narratives relating to different transnational and transcultural viewers in their respective localities and subjective contexts, to consider what got them deeply involved in a certain K-drama. In addition, I hope to clarify how transnational viewers beyond Asia are even more receptive toward K-dramas, how they try to understand K-dramas' stories and characters, and how this process compares with senses of identification from other international TV series, including dramas from the United States, the United Kingdom, and telenovelas.

UNIVERSAL THEME: ROMANCE IN K-DRAMAS

Storytelling typically suggests the centrality of narrative events whereas a story tells us about "what happens" (Mittell 2015, 259). In TV serials, storytelling is presented in a composition of four elements: a narrated story world, characters, events, and narrative sequences. The central function of storytelling is to increase the sense of continuity in the TV serials, connecting all these four elements to complete a story world. Above all, a TV series presents one story world where characters remember previous events and a set of relational episodes between characters and events are networked with the chronological order until the ending. The popularity of TV serials among television audiences is rooted in the cumulative impact of correlated narrative events, so viewers expect strict continuity and consistency within the narrative, in sync with the same mode of storytelling (Mittell 2015, 23). In terms of my interviews with Asian American K-drama viewers back in 2011, when asked what they like about K-dramas, these Korean TV fans mentioned the novel textual format, romantic storyline, and production quality. Some fans get used to the narrative elements, plots, and visual features of K-dramas, such that their comments indicate differences of K-drama's narrative composition from other foreign genres, which can be perceived as K-drama's mode of storytelling. It seems this mode of storytelling became the natural sensibility of K-drama when transnational viewers have constantly watched. For example, a female (Interviewee A, an Asian American college student) said, "I don't know. (laughing) But they're just so addictive. It's entertaining. I mean they're fun to watch and they're entertaining" (Interviewee A, personal interview with the author, April 2, 2011).

Alongside a storytelling mode, K-dramas have produced a peculiar story world on which to pin a specific narrative form in terms of Korean cultural and symbolic elements, which has been identified as the resource of emotional appeals distanced from other foreign TV series. First, the most common and popular theme in K-dramas is romance, highlighting the value of true love manifested by the ways of innocent sensibility, which are often seen as rare and unrealistic conditions in our tough world and complex reality (Han 2017; Ju and Lee 2015). Based on several ethnographic studies (see Hong-Mercier 2013; Hübinette 2012; Ju and Lee 2015; Kim 2013; Oh 2015; Otmazgin and Lyan 2013), transnational viewers of K-dramas have absorbed the love theme of K-dramas and have been entertained most by a culturally encoded love sentiment garnered from many episodes of the famous K-dramas. Indeed, transnational viewers and television critics have commented that the love themes of a majority of K-dramas aren't likely to show any kind of extreme, outrageous, or sarcastic depictions of love. Rather, the K-drama focuses more on developing a gentle and sincere romance apart from blatant sexual chemistries, gestures, violence, or immoral behaviors (de Castilho 2015). It is a cliché of the Korean romance drama that a love story infuses a bright sense of humor, hope, and sacrifice despite bittersweet and even sorrowful lifelike events. Moreover, romantic characters in K-dramas are constructed sensitively to identify and naturally express a wide spectrum of emotions about innocent love, scene by scene.

Second, characters are a central point in drawing viewers' minds to a dramatic narrative, so TV viewers usually develop a strong sense of intimacy with a drama series when they identify closely with a particular character or a favorite character's personality. In this regard, TV audiences can recall well the storyline of a drama serial based on their preferred character and his/her characteristic traits. Typically, TV romance viewers zero in on the leading characters, but the supporting characters in Korean romance narratives play more than trivial generic roles. In fact, these supporting characters often either provide a great support or a serious challenge to the leading characters' romance. For instance, if the leading characters' love is challenged mainly due to their social class differences, then the supporting characters may endeavor to widen this gulf by showing off a privileged social hierarchy (Ju 2019).

Third, Korean romance dramas utilize a particular narrative norm to establish a dramatic love theme, innocent emotions, gradually growing feelings of love, and ultimately relationships against the background of meddling life circumstances, social conflict, value standards, generational differences, speedy urbanization, and pro-commercial working environments within Korean society. Transnational viewers get more familiar with the prototype of Korean romance stories as they access a series of K-dramas, securing a new experience compared to the puzzling and entangled love stories notably produced by U.S. or Western style soap operas. When asked about transnational viewers' feelings for K-dramas, Interviewee B (female college student, Asian American) responded:

> I didn't even think the storyline matter! I don't really like to watch action or adventure one. I just want to watch like romantic, comedies or school-oriented kind of so. [sic] . . . when I first watch it, feel relax and calm. I usually watch it, sometimes I wish my life is like that. It kind of motivates me in a way that maybe I start doing that now. Umm . . . yes, I do. I guess that's why I'd like to watch Korean dramas. Takes me away from the real world or can escape from the real world. (Interviewee B, personal interview with the author, April 18, 2011)

By watching Korean romance dramas, transnational viewers can escape into romantic fantasy, but at the same time think about the situated reality surrounding them. Indeed, the popular K-dramas usually incorporate a contrasting plot, which is juxtaposed to the main romance narrative and contains versatile settings associated with real-life contexts, in order to make a good balance between realism and surreal romance. This mode of storytelling in Korean romance dramas allows many viewers not only to accept the predictable plot but also dream of a romantic fantasy, as they grow increasingly curious about an imagined Korea. In Korean romance narratives, networked and complex human relationships form important subplots, which draw viewers more into the realistic circumstance of the presented romance as another way of engaging with an unknown Korea and its living culture.

Overall, K-dramas generally produce a romance-forefront narrative, but the emphasis of subplots as well as the valued roles of supporting characters facilitate the supplemental narrative, which covers up the simplicity of the romance plot to produce a somewhat entangled and complex version of the story. Subplots commonly deal with complex issues in the lives of young adults, especially familial and social conflict, gender and class inequality, enormous competition for professional achievement, and hopes for prosperity. Both the complexity between characters and their entangled subplots remain a constant point of contact in each episode to create unpredictable emotional tensions alongside the usual romance narrative.

It is true, though, that many K-dramas continue to present a similar romance narrative as their central theme without radical transformation. An anonymous viewer's Netflix review of *Padam Padam* discusses this point:

> Beautifully written, filmed, directed and acted! Will make you angry, happy, joyful and sad all at the same time. Han Ji Min, Jung Woo Sung, Kim Bum and the actress who played lead characters mom were awesome! Be sure to have tissues available because you will be on an emotional roller-coaster ride that does not stop but you don't want it to end either! I really loved this series and will definitely watch it again!
>
> (Review of K-drama, *Padam Padam* on Netflix, February 2016)

As shown above, viewers can experience combined emotional scenes by navigating their preferred characters' stories. These characters create the momentum to engage in the narrative more deeply, getting the viewer voluntarily involved in enriching the original story to form alternative stories of the viewer's self-hypothesis as a means of pleasure.

In sum, the romance trope of the popular K-drama has changed little over the years since being recognized as the key feature of transnational K-dramas. The quintessential narrative norm of Korean romance dramas has continued to reproduce based on an inner cycle of TV production conventions among Korean TV producers, who create and recreate Korean TV storytelling by pinning diverse symbolic and generic narrative elements. Either a narrative or structural similarity among the popular K-dramas leads audiences to anticipate even a small variation from older to newer dramas. As such, even a little change between K-dramas is still noteworthy because the variations in situated events, characters (both leading and supporting), and degrees of conflict between characters also generate a different story world, where many viewers can engage in the emerging emotions. Specifically, small variations of Korean romance dramas have taken for granted modifications of characters' prototypes, situational events and settings, well-preserved subplots, and audiovisual effects. More or less, the common romance tropes have advanced the sophisticated textual and emotional elements as a modification to differentiate one drama to another, and most importantly this modification focuses on creating or provoking a fresh feeling of dramatic tension and a subtle sense of romantic appeal.

It is fair to say that K-dramas are consumed by viewers across national borders due to not only universal but also culture-anchored romance narratives. One K-drama fan, who participated in the *Goblin* viewing event arranged by DramaFever.com, said back in 2017: "Those [Korean drama stories] are very universal stories. They don't have to be Korean. I think they [US TV] picked good stories to remake, so more power to them. And if people are interested in the original, they can come to DramaFever" (Bai 2017). In sum, the Korean drama has built a culturally unique narrative that emphasizes a specific romance plot arc, conveying strong emotional appeals that are distinctive from other Asian or American romance stories, and transnational K-drama viewers are interested in this particular narrative form a lot more than other elements in K-dramas.

KOREAN ROMANCE NARRATIVES: THE PROTOTYPE AND CULTURAL SENTIMENT

At first glance, the archetypical Korean romance narrative reproduces and adapts Western fairy tale arcs, such as the Cinderella story, but the difference in Korean romance arises from many versions of modern events and symbolic appeals. The classic narrative structure of fairy tales is recreated in a modern urban love story involving characters with different family and social backgrounds. Most Korean romance dramas have a concrete ending within twenty-four episodes. Although some viewers complain about the slow progression of the love relationship between protagonists, compared to the pace in Western drama series, viewers of K-dramas enjoy a feasible resolution for that love. By viewing a completed love story in a drama, viewers experience much satisfaction and deeper emotional catharsis by the end of the show:

> American shows are really annoying sometimes. I think one thing about Asian dramas said that there's an end. American one, there's ten season or millions but Asian dramas are only one season or two seasons and there's an end. There's more resolution. (Interviewee A, personal interview with the author, April 2, 2011)

As many transnational audiences have mentioned, in the popular romance narrative of Korean romance dramas, a wealthy male hero falls in love with a poor heroine. In K-dramas, it is quite common that the male hero is a young CEO at one of Korea's top corporations, while the heroine is typically a young, bright, and charming woman belonging to the poor or middle class. Generally, this love story begins with an accidental encounter between the two protagonists and then they get more involved with each other through a series of coincidental events. K-dramas well-known among different transnational viewers, such as *Lovers in Paris*, *Secret Garden*, *Boys Over Flowers*, and *Heirs*, all share this romance trope. More and more Korean romance dramas continue to follow this love theme and narrative mode due to its international success, and many transnational viewers who are familiar with these K-drama narrative traits constantly seek out dramas conveying similar narrative tropes and love sentiments. While transnational viewers know that the main characters won't change extensively in terms of their basic nature and features, they do enjoy just a small change in the main characters, particularly the male protagonist, in a new romance drama. Different characterizations of the main characters are used to employ different situational contexts, professions, and personalities, enabling transnational viewers to feel differently about a new drama modeled after older ones. Another female interviewee, Interviewee C (college student, Asian American) made this point well: "That's why I like it [Korean drama]. You know, what the sweet things and romance that stuff [so] I can relate more [to Korean drama]" (Interviewee C, personal interview with the author, April 22, 2011).

Often, small changes in the male lead in Korean romance dramas produce different entertainment sources for viewers by tweaking the character's profession and personality a little. An innovative example of this narrative variation involves a love story with a specific romance between a celebrity male hero and a noncelebrity heroine. This modification of the main characters retains a dramatic conflict that challenges the characters' love relationship in association with their public identity, instead of with a contrasting class setting (e.g., wealth versus poor) as in the prototype of K-dramas. For instance, *You Are Beautiful*, *Oh! My Lady*, and *The Greatest Love* are all romance dramas that recreate different environmental challenges to the main characters' romantic union. In this case the class division, formerly a major conflict in the romance plot, has been replaced by the difference in social publicity between the main characters. It can be seen that both narratives are in line with the same locus of storytelling, so viewers can pleasurably recall earlier narratives when watching later dramas. In short, many Korean TV dramas focusing on romance storytelling share similar textual and narrative elements that motivate transnational viewers to discern the commonality as well as the difference, in tandem with intertextual reading practices comparing the new drama to the previous one. This feature plays an instrumental role in enhancing the overall translatability of K-dramas due to their similar narrative structure, which has made viewers likely to return to a kind of romance drama. The majority of transnational viewers frequently mention that they become addicted to K-dramas, especially romance narratives, after watching their first drama.

Moreover, digital technologies enable transnational viewers to extend their participation to a variety of foreign television stories, building voluntary communities around a drama story so they can enjoy an extended narrative universe of their own, beyond the original drama (Mittell 2015). A drama's romantic repertoires, such as images, artifacts, characters, theme music, and events, offer culturally signified narratives as the formula to portray a sense of love. More importantly, this romantic narrative formula originates from and is cultivated by Korea's domestic cultures and sentiment. Transnational viewers can therefore gain a specific cultural sense from Korean romance dramas apart from their own culture, and they can be entertained while exploring this specific cultural repertoire and symbolic context. Through online communities, fans of K-dramas across the world resonate well with the common romance narratives that make such an impact on these fans' worlds of K-dramas.

TRANSCULTURAL STORYTELLING: GENDER, CLASS, AND RACIAL/ETHNIC IMAGES

As discussed, the romance narrative of K-dramas looks sweet and has a good balance between the main plot and subplots. While the main plot focuses on developing the leading characters' love relationship, sometimes multiple subplots produce a variety of dramatic events, fueling natural context for the main plot. Again, the subplot relates more to realistic personal life stories than the main romance plot, and thus incorporates the interplay of current social backgrounds in Korea for viewers to comprehend. The drama thereby produces a central entertaining point: viewers see how the main characters' feelings grow, episode by episode. The essence of Korean romance narratives blends an ideal romance between the protagonists with their relatable day-to-day lives, given Korea's domestic norms that contain strong ideological values, even in defining the meaning of love. More or less, romantic love in Korea is associated with tensions over social class, familial relationships, ideology, and different life experiences. In other words, the love relationship in Korea does not simply relate to the private boundaries of the individual; rather, it is associated with complex human relations. In this respect, Korean romance dramas explore vivid senses of social conflict against the two protagonists' desire to be together.

John Fiske (1988, 247) claimed that one source of pleasure among TV viewers is the identification of a character: "The viewer makes meanings and pleasures from television that are relevant to his or her social allegiances at the moment of viewing." When viewers make more sense of the particular context of a narrative, the relevance of the narrative texts strengthens and focuses more on deeper meanings rather than superficial perception. Interviewee B substantiates this: "I guess the way it [a Korean drama] says basically different storylines. It's always different storyline. It says different things to me. I don't really think that it's the same storyline" (Interviewee B, personal interview with the author, April 18, 2011).

In light of contemporary TV criticism, melodrama or romance series seem like inherently feminine texts connecting to a viewer's biological sense and cultural norms. However, Jason Mittell refutes this view and asserts that romance dramas create a specific narrative impact that appeals more to female viewers and is pertinent to females' general thoughts and practices. From this point of view, females' romance drama consumption doesn't stem from a gender identity or a biological sense itself, but more from the particular mode of storytelling in TV romance narratives that produce strong ties with female viewers (Mittell 2015). Korean romance dramas are generally consistent with this tendency, as several empirical studies on K-drama consumption find that they more often communicate transnationally with female viewers than with male viewers.

Overall, there is a consensus among transnational viewers of K-dramas that the storytelling of Korean romance narratives presents sophisticated detail regarding the emotion of love and the people in a love relationship, so a highly sensitive affection is the central narrative element in developing the main plot. Specifically, early episodes of Korean romance dramas spend a relatively long time showing the acknowledged but uncertain love feelings between a hero and a heroine. This prepares for the male hero's subsequent sweet and comic actions, designed to increase the heroine's attention to him in everyday life, exhibiting the surge of his love for the heroine. He behaves sensitively to care for the heroine, even in the small parts of her daily routine, and his caring behavior touches her heart and prompts her to admit the feelings and relationship between the two of them. For example, in the drama *Go Back Couple*, on one rainy day the male protagonist waits for the heroine, hoping to "accidentally" meet her on campus. He eventually finds her on the street without an umbrella and approaches her naturally, putting his umbrella above her so they can share it. As they walk, he holds the umbrella over her side more than his side until they get to her destination. During this scene, the camera produces close-up shots of his wet shoulder, gently moving toward his subtle smile (see figure 2.1).

Figure 2.1 The Scene for a Romance Narrative: Sharing an Umbrella. *Source*: Screenshot by the author, the drama *Go Back Couple* (KBS, 2017).

Indeed, many Korean romance dramas have used a similar scene to portray the two characters' earliest love feelings. Such scenes touch the hearts of many female viewers, making them feel the sweet and tender side of love. Viewers could be captivated by the sensitive romantic mood and relate to the male's soft and caring characteristics. Moreover, this kind of caring action by a male protagonist gives female viewers comfort and openness to love, giving them time to get more excited about the couple's love relationship in future episodes. Without portraying immediate sexual activities, Korean romance dramas convey the nervous tension of love through elaborate emotional scenes. Interviewee C again stressed the romance narratives of K-dramas:

> For the most part, the American series are always like sex or drugs, stuff like that. The clothes are always revealing stuff like that. Okay. It's explosion, you know, boom boom boom. It's only the sexual concept of the thing. But Korean dramas, it's not all about the sexual thing. He loves her because he's in love with her, with sexual reasons like that. I feel like, for the most part in the American movies, [it's] like that. It's all the same thing, you know. (Interviewee C, personal interview with the author, April 22, 2011)

Asian actors have rarely been cast as romantic heroes and heroines in American TV series (Hogarth 2013), and in fact such Asian characters are rarely charming. In contrast, the romantic heroes and heroines of K-dramas present novel and positive images of Asians, and both their behaviors and interactions reject the stereotype that the Western drama series often create. Because of this charm, Korean romance dramas are well-received by both Asian and non-Asian viewers: Asian viewers want to identify with more favorable images of themselves, while non-Asian viewers want to explore the differences and freshness of unfamiliar roles for lead characters in the romance narrative.

Janice Radway (1983, 64) argued in her study of romance reading that female romance readers determine their active engagement in a certain romance story depending on the characterization of the male hero: "The quality of the ideal romantic fantasy is directly dependent on the character of the heroine and the manner in which the hero treats her. [. . .] A good romance involves an unusually bright and determined woman and a man who is spectacularly masculine, but at the same time capable of remarkable empathy and tenderness." Her analysis illustrates that female readers expect to identify with the heroine when reading a romance, so a male hero should treat the heroine nicely. To maximize readers' anticipation or pseudo-experience in a romance, the male hero should possess a more nurturing personality along with a physically strong, masculine body. Not all, but many male characters in Korean romance dramas share identical personalities and physical features. More importantly, K-dramas' male characters are often shown as more capable of sensitive, caring, and selfless behaviors, so in that sense, they appear gently handsome in contrast with strong and powerful masculine figures (Ju and Lee 2015; Kim 2013; Lin and Tong 2008).

More precisely, male protagonists in K-dramas are depicted kindly and identified as stylish and soft masculine figures in a series of romantic event scenes as the drama's romance plot advances. For instance, the drama *Secret Garden* is known by many transnational (or even domestic) viewers for one greatly popular scene between the male (Hyun Bin) and female (Ha Jiwon) leads that aired in one of its early episodes. In the scene, Hyun Bin was eager to meet Ha Jiwon again after a coincidental encounter, so he visited a training class where she was teaching fellow stunt actors. Even though she did not welcome him, Hyun Bin behaved like a regular student during the training program. When they practiced a warming-up exercise, he asked to be her training partner given the other fellows' silent support, though she was very embarrassed. However, he performed the routine naturally, listening carefully to her instructions just like the other regular fellows. At one point he lay on the floor with both knees raised, doing sit-ups to strengthen his stomach muscles. His partner Ha Jiwon held his knees tightly, so their faces came

Figure 2.2 A Scene from a Romance Narrative: *Secret Garden*. *Source*: Screenshot by the author, the drama *Secret Garden*.

close together during the up-and-down motion of the exercise. Suddenly, he stopped halfway through the exercise and stared at her softly. She averted her eyes in response, even as his face got closer (see figure 2.2). This scene touched many female viewers, particularly in terms of how romantic the hero is and how the scene portrayed a sweet, loving mood. In fact, this scene became so popular among fans and viewers that they often discuss their own emotions when watching the scene. Several parody videos of the scene have also appeared online.

To intensify the romantic mood based on emotional closeness, male characters' facial and body images appear as soft and gentle in many Korean romances, and men are often represented with a different masculine image that emphasizes tenderness, a cute face, and a nice body even without physical strength. In scene after scene, the focus is on their sweet facial expressions, eye contact, and tender gestures. This way of presenting the male characters seems more effective in delivering a personality emphasizing tender hearts and strong minds. Such an approach contrasts starkly with the male characters in Western TV series, who are more often presented with strong and powerful body images along with a highly confident personality.

Previous studies of K-dramas have described male characters in terms of a soft masculinity formed by the moral maturity of the adult male, rather than the physical masculinity of the sexual body. Transnational viewers of K-dramas often appreciate the male characters' sensitive, soft, noble, and gentle personalities more than their physical attractiveness (Jung 2011). In particular, female viewers articulate their pleasure in seeing such distinguished male characters. It provides a novel quality to Korean romance dramas in comparison to Western soap operas or melodramas, as this Netflix review documents:

I have never binge watched a TV series and then started from the very beginning and watch it all over again as soon I finished the first viewing. This show is that good. [. . .] I guess it is a cultural thing, this type of romance rarely vibes in the States. But this show. Love the actors, love characters, the chemistry is just explosive and the little twist about switching bodies is perfect. It does not dominate the show instead adds to its quirkiness. [. . .] And Hyun Bin character, love his manner, he just comes out says whatever. It's perfect. The pacing is great, the show never loses momentum. I recommend this for anyone looking for a light-hearted romance, some good comedic fun and wanting to try something different. [5 stars, 2 helpful]

(Review of K-drama, *Secret Garden* on Netflix, February 2016)

Interestingly, the romance cliché in K-drama narratives, as discussed above, draws special attention among transnational viewers in terms of the sense of class hierarchy between lovers. Many romance dramas, though not all, utilize the social class ideology of Korean society as a metaphor to challenge the couple's love relationship. Many fans, regardless of nationality, rapidly recognize and actively engage in discussions of class struggles within K-drama narratives. It seems that transnational viewers try to interpret this particular ideology in the domestic culture as a negotiated decoding relating to their local culture and ideological position (Han 2017). Class hierarchy in K-dramas is commonly described as a division of wealthy versus poor, elite versus non-elite, or white collar versus blue collar. While the foregrounded image of Korea in many dramas is very much a romanticized nation as well as an industrialized, urbanized, and democratic country, the class hierarchy that these dramas convey reflects contemporary Korea beyond its cool and affluent national heritage. In this sense, viewers seem more critically engaged with the high-power characters (e.g., parents, bosses, prestigious politicians, conservative scholars, etc.), who play a realistic role in elaborating the diversified ideologies of the nation.

From the viewer's point of view, Korean romance dramas that portray class divisions bring up divergent opinions and critiques about whether it is a fictional tool or not. By doing so, some viewers more actively translate the embedded meanings of sharp and conscious class divisions and note surprise over how deeply Korean people and society are divided over class ideologies. Asian viewers take it for granted as a more realistic portrait of Korea because their countries also have this homologous social structure. But both Asian and non-Asian viewers find a mixed sense of otherness from Korea in association with this domestic ideological narrative. Interviewee C said, "Even though it [Korean TV] looks modern, it still looks like more traditional thing and it's more conservative than the American one" (Interviewee C, personal interview with the author, April 22, 2011).

As a result, broad and straightforward depictions of class divisions in K-drama narratives are effective to emulate the romantic fantasy, but simultaneously this cultural narrative widens the foreign sensibility toward K-dramas among transnational viewers. At some point, the sense of foreignness may be a new source of pleasure as well as a cultural window to reveal a shadow of the real Korea.

K-DRAMA VIEWERS' RITUALS

Viewers are hooked by a TV series due to narrative elements, but these elements accelerate the viewer's active involvement in meaning making through emotional and behavioral engagement practices. Some recent studies on TV fandom suggested that social media fosters discursive and communicative practices of many drama viewers and that these collective activities in different social media extend the pleasure of watching the drama (Oh 2015). Viewers who are more likely to participate in fan communities for a certain TV drama series seek different paratextual activities[1] to deeply comprehend the drama and drama-related contextual information. As part of these paratextual practices, point-to-point discussions about a drama series encourage community members to decode the narrative with multiple versions of their own ideas and also encourage a recreation of favorite characters to behave differently from the original storyline in the drama by means of utilizing fan fictions or fan-edit episode videos. For fans of a drama series, this type of engagement in an online fan community lets them be more active in the imagery, storyline, and characters for their own pleasure. In addition, many fans in different TV drama communities note that mutual involvement in decoding or translating specific textual meanings for a particular episode or a drama text can deepen their empathy and pleasures, in ways that might not be so motivated when watching the show alone.

K-dramas' common narratives, especially in the romance dramas, contribute to establishing certain behaviors of intertextual readings and intermediary consumption. Both behavior patterns are closely associated with cult fan communities for a specific form of narrative, and behavioral engagement by both TV viewers and fans enrich in-depth and critical reception to a particular TV show or other media form. Chalaby (2016b) claimed that drama series, as scripted shows, generally have more difficulty crossing national borders because not only does drama need to resonate more deeply than unscripted shows, but the success of a drama series is more dependent on viewers' deep and critical reception. Previously, several audience studies of K-dramas in different regions explored how viewers outside of Korea consumed K-dramas to feed their cultural tastes and to revisit their affection for continuing to watch similar K-dramas. In other words, transnational viewers who liked the drama *Winter Sonata*[2] also enjoyed dramas such as *Autumn Fairy Tales*, *Stairways to Heaven*, *Beautiful Days*, and *All In*, all of which sketch out a love story of heartbreak. Likewise, transnational viewers who liked brighter romantic comedies, such as *Boys Over Flowers*, also preferred *You're Beautiful*, *Full House*, *Coffee Prince*, and *Heirs*, all of which emphasize unexpected love encounters.

Viewers who are familiar with Korean romance narratives can expect similar narrative norms to be adopted in other romance series, so these viewers are well aware how they would engage with some points of a new story as well as with new characters' behaviors. When transnational viewers explore culturally different audiovisual content, these viewers continue to watch similar lines of narratives that they've enjoyed, in order to increase their pleasure by means of revealing differences and commonalities between similar textual forms. This tendency is defined as inclusive cultural consumption (Otmazgin and Lyan 2013).

According to Scheulze (2013, 373), transnational fans of K-dramas establish their own translated K-drama world called "K-dramaland." The term is used among international fans to produce active discussions and interpretative practices that generate a deep understanding of the narrative, created by the collective activity of writers, directors, and actors. Discursive online communications by fans regarding K-dramaland include explanations about characters' peculiar cultural and/or social behaviors, as well as discursive opinions that contribute to crystalizing K-dramaland rules: narrative norms of how characters are to behave or to react in the common K-drama. Through K-dramaland discussions, it is certain that transnational fans gain necessary, in-depth knowledge about K-dramas' narrative formulas—knowledge that furthermore motivates these fans to intensely participate in different paratextual activities. Thus, K-dramaland serves as a site for making sense of the K-drama's specific story world through active involvement and discursive communication, and this enables transnational fans to generate advanced pleasures sourced from the dramatic narratives they like.

Overall, pop culture consumers who are willing to be enthusiastic fans of a particular content rarely hesitate to try and experience another similar type of cultural content. This explains, to a certain degree, how several Korean romance dramas with seemingly analogous storylines constantly gain the attention of transnational viewers.

NOTES

1. The Internet has emerged as an active site for discursive reactions and interactions about television programs, so paratextual practices have become more important

in contemporary TV fandom studies. Using paratexts, TV viewers often participate in extra activities to be better informed or more deeply engaged with certain TV shows, especially TV dramas or serials. For instance, a TV viewer might visit online discussion sites, fan wikis, or Twitter conversations, or search for spoilers in the moments before, during, or after watching a drama. Various paratextual practices substantially change the viewer's comprehension of the TV drama or serial narratives (Mittell 2015).

2. *Winter Sonata* is a Korean TV drama that garnered huge transnational popularity among many Asian audiences in the early 2000s, and the Korean Wave spread broadly throughout Asia due to this drama's popularity and commercial success. It is a love story composed of a twisted plot that includes an unforgettable memory about first love. In 2002, this twenty-four-episode drama was broadcast via KBS-2, which is a terrestrial TV channel owned by the KBS. The director, Yoon Seok-Ho, produced it as the second of his four seasonal love story serials. *Winter Sonata* recorded a 24.5 percent average TV rating when it first aired in Korea. Although this rating wasn't the highest in Korea at the time, *Winter Sonata* came to be more popular than other competitors scheduled in the same time slot because of the main characters, impressive casts, and the overall plot twists. Based on the drama's controversy as well as avid viewers' feedback, it achieved huge commercial success, including the export of broadcast rights to sixteen countries throughout Asia between 2003 and 2005. The drama produced passionate female fandoms in Japan in particular, and Japan later became a major importer of many other Korean TV dramas. Both the drama's original soundtrack and the main characters' fashion products became the trendiest items in many Asian countries when the drama was broadcast through their local TV channels. The actors who played the drama's title roles, Bae YongJoon and Choi JiWoo, were likewise selected as two of the most beloved Asian actors and especially in Japan they remain big stars.

Chapter 3

Korean TV Shows with East Asian Partnership

The East Asian cultural milieu has changed significantly since 2000, especially as the media and entertainment industry embraced more regional collaboration and cooperative interactions. It is well noted that East Asian countries have been inspired by rapidly growing transnational flows of media and pop culture, and under this new media environment television dramas contribute significantly to pinning regional cultural exchanges as a counter-flow of the Western media's penetration. Without diluting their national and/or cultural identity, television dramas imported from close neighbors have proven to cater better to wide-ranging domestic audiences across East Asia. Japanese TV dramas are a good example of this trend. Despite strict broadcast regulations by national governments designed to protect each nation's unique culture and identity, these dramas successfully moved into different East Asian TV channels during the 1990s. Shortly after, both Taiwan and Hong Kong allowed the official broadcast of Japanese TV dramas on their domestic channels.

Nonetheless, Korea and China officially banned Japanese TV broadcasts on their television channels a decade longer than other East Asian nations. China has strict governmental control on domestic broadcasting and foreign media imports, regulated by the Chinese Communist Party, so this policy is not just for Japanese television programs. By contrast, the Korean government retained an official ban on inflows of Japanese television programs until 2004, mainly to avoid unfavorable cultural influence from its former colonizer (Ju 2014).

As discussed in chapter 1, the Korean Wave has demonstrated an evolving process over the past two decades, featuring growing speed and scope, disseminated geographies, and new media impacts on consumption by transnational audiences. Meanwhile, Korean TV drama has enjoyed record-breaking success and was consumed in many parts of Asia, although its huge popularity within Asia has waned a little. However, Korean dramas have attracted even broader international audiences, spreading farther into the Middle East, North and South America, and Europe since 2010, in accordance with the global K-pop boom (Hong 2013; Jin 2016; Kim 2015; Lie 2012). Some scholars take a skeptical view of the Korean Wave, claiming that, despite its peak drive to global success, Korean dramas' conservative nature and a lack of creativity now point to stagnation in its global distribution (Ainslie et al. 2017, 65–66).

It is certainly worth noting that the desire for better industrial profits among Korean broadcasting corporations has greatly increased in the age of the Korean Wave, so Korean broadcasters take it for granted that their homegrown content will go abroad as usual. As East Asian countries have established modernization and globalization at concurrent times, despite varying time lapses in each country, this advanced modern milieu across the region has brought about high commonality on each country's domestic trajectories for social, economic, and cultural dimensions. Given this collective Asian experience, the mediated Korean dramas contribute to respectful representations of East Asian modern cultures, lifestyles, and identities that many East Asian viewers can admit and respond to positively. In this vein, the flow of Korean TV dramas enables East Asian regional media to resurrect their creative resources for content production, targeting the burgeoning TV industry abroad (Yasumoto 2014).

Further, this process boosts the East Asian media industry in terms of the regional media's interpenetration, using their respective TV content and the related creative markets. Thus, the East Asian media industry (including Korean television) has, to a certain degree, strengthened its mutual bonds of coproduction, joint-venture investment, and broadcast partnerships. To examine this phenomenon in more depth, this chapter outlines the reciprocal phase of the East Asian television industry's development alongside transnational Korean dramas and then showcases some exemplary TV dramas based on East Asian media firms' collaboration to examine the meanings of regional production and distribution. More importantly, it investigates and discusses Korean broadcasters' relationships with both China and Japan, with regard to their regional media initiatives and active market creation surrounding popular Korean dramas within the region.

A REGIONAL DRAMA, *METEOR GARDEN*

In the fall of 1999, *Big Brother* was broadcast for the first time in the Netherlands, shaking media audiences all over Europe. Shortly after the first run on Dutch TV Endemol, the original Dutch producer of *Big Brother* sold the format to other European countries, including Germany, Australia, Belgium, Denmark, Greece, Italy, Norway, Portugal, Poland, Spain, the United Kingdom, Switzerland, and Sweden (Zoonen 2001). *Big Brother* quickly became a huge hit internationally, driven by viewers' contrasting opinions on the show's new live-production style: it was a surprise for a TV show to portray the characters' daily lives, based on surveillance of a group of people living ordinary lives (Zoonen 2001). Many agree that *Big Brother* was the first TV show to launch the so-called "reality show" productions, inaugurating global television's discovery of the age of reality TV shows. In the United States, the CBS network obtained the format and aired the first season under the same title *Big Brother* in 2000. It is still being broadcast, currently in its twentieth season.

Big Brother has enjoyed almost mythical success as a European show, developing a popular TV format which earned international recognition as a fresh and locally adaptable TV show. Similarly, the TV drama *Meteor Garden* draws attention to the regional TV format that was repeatedly adopted and remade within the East Asian television industry. *Meteor Garden*, an original Taiwanese TV drama, emphasizes the important interpenetration of an East Asian TV drama among regional broadcasters during the 2000s. Even though this drama's popularity was restricted to Asia, unlike *Big Brother*, it triggered a rising trend of inter-Asian content production and distribution, so it has been acknowledged as birthing the regional TV format in East Asian television industries.

In 2000, a Taiwanese television station purchased *Meteor Garden*'s original story from a Japanese manga, *Hana yori dango*, to remake it into a television drama. The original manga had established a solid fan base in both Taiwan and other Asian countries (Iwabuchi 2002). Drawing on the existing fandom for the original story, *Meteor Garden* was a romantic comedy focusing on four vivid male characters—all belonging to a privileged social class—and their comic adventures at a private university in Taiwan. The male leads functioned as celebrities at the university, the envy of ordinary students. By contrast, the female protagonist was an ordinary tomboy with a friendly personality, distinguishing herself from the cold and arrogant male leads. The class struggle among them became a focal point of the entire story. As the plot advanced, all four men showed interest in the heroine, but only one ended up falling in love with her; in the meantime, the four male characters bonded together and used their strong friendship to support the new couple.

Meteor Garden was an instant success when it was screened in Hong Kong, Singapore, and Korea later in 2002. Viewers in these countries liked the funny and dramatic narratives, but most of all they liked the four attractive male leads, dubbed *F4*. Prior to this drama, all four of the F4 actors were completely unknown young actors in Taiwan, but once it aired, every one of their public appearances drew huge crowds of screaming fans. After the domestic broadcast of *Meteor Garden* in Taiwan ended, in fact, the actors created a F4 band to extend their characters from the drama, becoming the first regional entertainers who effectively adopted their dramatic images for music stardom. The Taiwanese media strategically utilized the F4 band to advertise *Meteor Garden* for promotional tours, concerts, and fan meetings in the major cities of East Asia and even a few in South Asia.

The sweeping regional popularity of *Meteor Garden* was an unexpected success for a national TV drama (Chua 2004), so the Taiwanese television industry wanted to take advantage of it. They quickly built commercial strategies to increase the export of the drama for either local remakes or exclusive local broadcasts before the quick popularity cycle of the drama dissipated among Asian viewers. The successful diffusion of popular foreign media is closely associated with immediate diffusion: "[TV] content is being exchanged or cloned so rapidly that there is an increasing sense of connectedness. Success in one market is very quickly transferred to another market" (Keane et al. 2007, 24). Taiwan had a relatively advanced cable television industry at the time, so the timely regional distribution of their popular dramas was planned and executed to target the region's viewers.

In response to Taiwanese broadcasters, the KBS, a public TV network, decided in 2008 to remake *Meteor Garden* into a Korean TV drama, retitled *Boys Over Flowers*. The Korean remake adopted a similar plot arc based on the original Taiwanese drama, but both the main setting and the F4 characters were modified to increase the male leads' attractiveness to the viewers (see figure 3.1). *Boys Over Flowers* was a twenty-episode comic romance

Figure 3.1 *Boys Over Flowers* **(Korea).** *Source*: Screenshot by the author, the intro of *Boys Over Flowers*.

stressing on class struggle and hierarchical ideology set in a prestigious high school in Korea, featuring a romance between the F4 leader and a cute, middle-class female lead getting along well with the other wealthy F4 members. In the Korean remake, the F4 characters were symbolic representatives of young Koreans from wealthy families, similar to the original Taiwanese drama, and their good looks and fashion-savvy style played a major factor in gaining a larger response within Korea and across Asia. The Korean F4 in *Boys Over Flowers* gained more popularity than the previous Taiwanese F4 when the drama was disseminated in different Asian countries as well as via streaming TV platforms. Lee Min-Ho, who played the Korean F4 leader, achieved Asian stardom as a result of the drama's success, leading to similar roles in later Korean dramas. Recently, for instance, his drama *Heirs* was named the best East Asian drama of 2016, based on viewers' online votes at the U.S. streaming website DramaFever.com (DramaFever.com 2017).

Boys Over Flowers demonstrates the commercial success of a specific TV remake based on the Korean romance drama norm. This phenomenon drives an emerging interest in the potency of East Asian television content that has long been archived in the origin country's national television. Both *Meteor Garden* and *Boys Over Flowers* earned significant commercial success using East Asian TV drama, drawing more attention to mutual TV exchanges among regional broadcasters. Moreover, *Boys Over Flowers* was positioned as a prototype of Korean romance dramas, particularly targeting international youth audiences with its emphasis on young, good-looking male characters and their sweet and gentle romantic interactions within relatable living conditions. For instance, many Asian viewers proclaim *You are Beautiful* and *The Rooftop Prince* as subsequent Korean dramas that incited similar pleasures to *Boys Over Flowers*.

In addition, the popularity of *Boys Over Flowers* within Asia and beyond called for the rebroadcast of *Meteor Garden* in both Taiwan and Korea (and even other countries such as China and Japan), at which avid fans of these dramas explored the two narratives via intermediary consumption from a comparative viewpoint. Chapter 6 will analyze the format of East Asian television and beyond in greater depth. In the following section, the regional media partnerships of Korean broadcasters, centered on the Korean drama production, is examined with relation to their mutual exchanges and collaborations with both Chinese and Japanese television corporations.

PARTNERSHIPS BETWEEN KOREAN AND CHINESE TELEVISION

During the 1980s, the Chinese television industry turned its broadcasting system into a commercial model that led them to highly focus on producing more TV entertainment than ever before, a commercial transformation maintained until the late 1990s (Bai 2005). Under this commercial model, Chinese television was flooded with a large volume of soap operas imported from Western and Japanese television. With the strong commercial drive of television stations in China, a large number of channels emerged to cover the large territory, similar to other countries' multichannel systems across East Asia.

Specifically, the Chinese television industry has classified multiple TV channels based on its ownerships and broadcast coverage; CCTV as a party-state TV channel is a state-owned terrestrial channel and there are provincial TV channels, provincial capital city channels, and lastly regional city channels in different provinces (Bai 2005). From the end of the 1990s to the early 2000s, some large provincial TV channels turned to satellite TV to broaden their broadcast coverage; for example, Hunan Satellite Television, the leading provincial satellite TV network, produces the most popular entertainment programs among national audiences (Bai 2005). In 2003, Hunan Satellite TV promoted itself as the first entertainment-oriented channel in China to build an image of youth, beauty, and fashion (Hunan TV homepage), an approach well-suited for a commercial broadcast model.

In the Chinese television system, television drama is definitely the primary entertainment show capable of establishing an advertising-based TV structure, and earlier analysis showed that prime-time dramas in China can bring up to 70 percent of a station's total advertising revenue (Bai 2005; Wang 2001). With this in mind, even the state-owned station, CCTV, increased the prime-time drama ratio on its flagship channel CCTV 1, going from a one-hour format to a two-hour format and increasing the number of daily episodes from two to eight (Bai 2005, 27). Meanwhile, Korean dramas aired via Chinese TV channels gained positive acclaim for their high production quality and fresh storylines, which was enough for them to replace other foreign imports from the United States and Japan. The changing media environment of Chinese television in the mid-2000s met the transnational flow of Korean dramas in a timely response to highly increasing demand for entertainment shows, mostly TV dramas, in the booming Chinese provincial and satellite television stations.

Notably, Chinese television resumed imports of Korean dramas in 2006 to feed their channels and to entice youth audiences who like to watch modern dramas from Japan or Korea. Due to increasing volumes of Korean dramas, Chinese broadcasters lamented the heavy influence of the Korean television industry, expressing concern with production and the deepening trade deficits. This brought a backlash against the Korean Wave in 2007 and 2008, especially driven by the Chinese government's new foreign TV broadcast quota that directly targeted Korean dramas. This new foreign TV quota required control of the foreign dramas' total airtime and limited the number of episodes to be aired per year (Ministry of Culture, Sports, and Tourism

2010). It was apparent that this enhanced broadcasting restriction strongly reduced Korean TV drama overseas exports at the time.

In a counter-initiative, the Korean television industry shifted its commercial approach to the Chinese television market. Industry players established partnerships with Chinese TV stations on a variety of levels, collaborating on both drama production and investment funding instead of just using finished TV program exchanges. In this way, Korean television stations created opportunities to coproduce TV dramas (and other entertainment programs) with Chinese TV stations. Korean independent production companies and Chinese provincial television or online media investment corporations also cooperated to fund future-release Korean dramas that needed a particularly big budget. Accordingly, the program trade between Korea and China has been diversified, including format trades (both for TV dramas and variety shows), direct sales of local TV broadcast and streaming online exclusive rights, and institutional coproduction projects. Above all, the two governments jointly drafted and signed the Free Trade Agreement in 2015, emphasizing the two countries' media partnerships. China decided to engage with Korean media systems on creative content production and distribution after seeing the popularity of transnational TV and film recently produced in Korea (Chua 2012; Iwabuchi 2013; Keane and Liu 2013; Jin and Yoon 2016).

All these methods for television programming, production, and trade have enriched both nations' TV industries and markets, making China one of Korea's most important media and cultural allies. The two countries are mutually interested in expanding their television and film coproduction and joint-venture systems. Chinese media practitioners, firms, and policymakers have likewise increasingly sought to boost the international appeal of Chinese media and pop culture by the integration of foreign competitors and collaborators (Yecies 2016).

Along with the policy change, another speedy transformation in the recent Chinese mediascape involves emerging online video (streaming only) sites, whose viewership among domestic viewers has rapidly increased year to year. This online viewership in China has greatly affected the influence of the Korean Wave on the young generation, who prefer to consume Korean dramas, though more recently Korean variety shows have also become more popular on Chinese online TV platforms. It has been well noted that the most famous domestic Korean television shows, even divided into short video forms, are almost simulcast via the major Chinese streaming sites such as Youku, Tudou, iQiyi, Sohu, and PPTV. Through these streaming sites the most updated Korean dramas are uploaded weekly and, in some cases, are simulcast to match the Korean domestic broadcast schedule (Ahn 2014). Some websites, in fact, stream those Korean TV shows without online broadcast copyrights, so it is worth noting that unauthorized online distribution channels in China have long been a huge problem in the realm of global media industry. This gets more complicated with the diversification of Chinese online media penetration. According to the Broadcasting Industry Report of the Korean Ministry of Science, ICT, and Future Planning (2016), the three main Chinese online sites have streamed approximately eighty licensed Korean variety shows. For example, Youku is streaming *I Can See Your Voice* and *Grandpa Over Flowers*, and iQiyi is running *Take Care of My Refrigerator*, *1 Night and 2 Days*, and *Running Man*. Sohu is streaming *Get it Beauty* (Ministry of Science, ICT and Future Planning 2016).

In terms of coproduction, the partnership between Korean and Chinese television has been actively developing in recent years due to changing policies and diplomatic relations between the two nations. The converging media environment in both countries, along with online and mobile platforms, also demonstrates the importance of a burgeoning new segment of online TV viewership. In this vein, Korean broadcasters and independent drama production firms have increased the number of dramas coproduced with Chinese media and entertainment companies. With this coproduction process, Korean drama (or variety show) scripts are adopted under the management of Korean TV stations or independent production firms. In many cases, Chinese media companies play an investing and promotional role in these coproduction projects, mostly to gain the exclusive broadcast rights for their local and provincial channels and for streaming TV, when the coproduced drama first airs. Another result of drama coproduction is that Chinese TV producers and program executives advance their own production know-how. The most successfully coproduced TV drama between Korea and China was the military romance *Descendants of the Sun*, which aired in 2016, so its coproduction is worth considering as an example of the two nations' successful new media partnership.

Descendants of the Sun finished shooting and editing its sixteen full episodes in 2015 and aired the following year via the KBS-2 channel in Korea; this was a rare case of completing all the episodes before the drama's first run. In Korean television, some Korean dramas have been produced in so-called "live-production" conditions, where all the episodes are filmed at the same time while the earlier episodes are airing, but *Descendants of the Sun* was an exception to that production convention. It was also the first simulcast drama on both Korean TV and Chinese streaming channels, in this case iQiyi, which had exclusive coverage in China (Wong 2016).

In terms of profits, after the first couple episodes aired in Korea and China, the drama was a megahit in both countries and was sold to TV broadcasters in thirty-two countries, including the United Kingdom, France, Italy, Germany, and Spain, along with many Asian buyers (Lee and Szalai 2016). IQiyi.com reported that the pilot was viewed more than one billion times on the platform during the simulcast. Thanks to its enormous popularity, *Descendants of the Sun* quickly paid off the entire production cost (approximately $11 million) that Chinese media firms had invested and sold all its advertising spots, including product placements. Specifically, iQiyi.com in China purchased the simultaneous streaming rights for $250,000 per episode, which was equivalent to almost 40 percent of the drama's entire production costs (Kang 2016).

As addressed, *Descendants of the Sun* was coproduced by a special production company (SPC) initiative, created between a Korean independent production firm, NEW, and KCGS, a public network's (KBS) subsidiary content firm. In this SPC coproduction system, NEW managed the entire production process, including casting actors, hiring writers and production crews, shooting, and editing. Meanwhile, KGCS managed the broadcasting schedule, domestic and foreign promotions, and broadcast licensing sales. Both NEW and KGCS invested half of the entire drama production budget in the preproduction stage, and the registered SPC for *Descendants of the Sun* signed an agreement to share 50 percent of the resulting profits from the total sales revenue of the finished drama. In the end, the drama's copyrights came to be owned by this SPC.

The SPC stimulated media content production, so the Korean government used it to develop an institutional policy for the creative content industry as an amendment of the Media and Cultural Industry Act in Korea. Since 2006, this policy has allowed the exclusive establishment of a SPC to produce media-related content for TV, film, performance arts, and pop culture as a limited periodic firm, upon legal registration with the Korean Ministry of Culture, Sports, and Tourism (Ministry of Culture, Sports, and Tourism 2012). Usually a SPC for media content is registered for one to three years until the entire production process ends. In addition, the government offers a tax benefit to SPCs for TV drama production (Ministry of Culture, Sports, and Tourism 2012; Yu and Moon 2014). Korean dramas using SPC production name their companies *Munhwa-Sanup-Jeonmun-Heoisa* (in Korean) preceded by the drama's title; for example, *Descendants of the Sun*'s SPC is DS Munhwa-Sanup-Jeonmun-Heoisa in Korean. All in all, the SPC system in Korean drama production specifically aims to implement an asymmetric TV production structure within the Korean television system. The media policymakers hoped to lessen the dominance of producing TV dramas by Korean network broadcasters to create a diversified and promotional TV drama production environment, especially by encouraging and supporting a various range of small and large independent production firms outside Korean TV networks (Ju 2017).

In the case of *Descendants of the Sun*, the main production firm, NEW, prepared the qualified script of the drama written by top Korean TV drama writer, Kim Eun-Sook, and also successfully cast two top Korean actors,

Song Joong-Ki and Song Hye-Kyo, for the drama's lead roles. When preproduction of the drama started in early 2015, NEW acquired an investment fund from both Huace Media Investment Corporation (Hong Kong-based) and Baidu's video-streaming affiliate iQiyi.com (Chinese media group). This Chinese media investment was facilitated, thanks to casting two top Korean Wave stars instead of the original script in the first place (Kang 2016). Chinese media firms' investment in *Descendants of the Sun* also meant that the Chinese governmental quotas on broadcasting foreign dramas could be eased (Wong 2016); furthermore, the drama's simulcast via iQiyi was heavily promoted through the major Chinese press. For instance, an editorial in *People's Daily*—the official press of the Chinese Communist Party—praised the drama as "an excellent advertisement for conscription," showcasing Korea's national spirit and communitarian culture. It also suggested that China should create a soap opera of similar quality (Wong 2016). In short, *Descendants of the Sun* shows the ways the Chinese media industry is involved in Korean television industry, highlighting the extent to which the Korean Wave contributes to the two nations' reciprocal collaboration in the realm of television.

PARTNERSHIPS BETWEEN KOREAN AND JAPANESE TELEVISION

Unlike Chinese television, the Japanese television industry is the most advanced media system within the East Asian region and even beyond. As previously noted, Japanese TV programs, especially dramas, TV animations, and music and entertainment shows, have been largely circulated throughout Asia. It should be noted that Japan has been recognized as a top-tier media industry rooted in Asia since the 1980s. Often, Japanese media content served to represent all East Asian media content in the Western media scene as the regional forerunner.

Iwabuchi (2004a, 23) asserted that foreign TV dramas were typically unable to gain prime time slots on Japanese television. Since 1990, few foreign TV dramas have been able to break that barrier, except for the U.S. series *The X-Files* in 1995. Japanese television audiences showed little enthusiastic responses to these foreign TV shows, as it was particularly hard for such programs to positively appeal to Japanese audiences (Lee and Ju 2010, 78). More significantly, the exchange of television content between Korea and Japan was more difficult because of the two countries' historical relationship. In 2004, the Korean government finally wrapped up the official policy that it had begun in 1998, unlocking its doors to a set of Japanese popular culture products such as movies, television programs, music, and animations. It removed restrictions on Japanese film and pop music that had been previously banned to those under the age of seventeen, while the broadcast of Japanese TV dramas had never been allowed on Korean television channels, including cable and satellite TV. The official openness policy took six years to be fully implemented before the Korean government allowed official inflows of Japanese media and pop culture products. It was a critical reversal of a decades-old restriction that had been in place since Korea's official liberation from Japanese colonial rule in 1945 (Lee 2008; Yasumoto 2014).

Along with this policy, Korean dramas began opening the door to Korean exchanges with the self-sufficient Japanese television system. The former popularity of Japanese TV dramas began to face new competition with the circulated Korean TV dramas across the whole Asian region. Japan, too, embraced Korean TV dramas more actively starting in 2002, and in 2003 *Winter Sonata*, the most popular show in Japan, actually broke the highest viewership record for foreign TV dramas. This clearly marked the arrival of the Korean Wave in Japan, and until 2012, Japan was the number one importer of Korean TV dramas based on the volumes being exported from Korea. The completion of Korea's open policy to Japanese media content notably concurred with an arrival of the Korean Wave in Japan at almost the same time, and the two country's television industries then began a new partnership in TV and music content production. According to Hayashi and Lee (2007), the Korean Wave has pushed forward a promotion for sharing media content, production systems, and human resources in creative content markets among East Asian nations. In addition, the Korea-Japan partnership in the television industry enriches the production resources, creative content mechanisms, and marketing know-how for distribution within the regional media industry. When asked what the Korean Wave implied for the Korean television industry, one Korean broadcast practitioner said this:

> In 2000, some dramas like *Winter Sonata* and *Daejanggeum* were exported to many other Asian countries. There was an enormous response to Winter Sonata, particularly by Japan, so this unpredicted event created momentum for the Korean broadcasting industry to be awakened about new values of our TV dramas. I think that the Korean Wave at the time made a real impact in the history of foreign business of the Korean program. Thanks to the unexpected success of *Winter Sonata* in Japan, the exportation of Korean dramas in the following years, from 2003 to 2005, increased up to 100 per cent annually in terms of its exported volume and revenue. Furthermore, the commercial success of Winter Sonata did create more privileged opportunity to other Hallyu-related business as followed, although the annual growth of drama exportation started decreasing slightly in 2006. To me, this tendency indicates that the effect of Winter Sonata is no longer a single stimulus to retain more success of Korean dramas overseas. But, I am very sure that the Korean Wave arrives the overall Asia and becomes a stable movement to create inroads for our TV dramas, regardless of a little

diminishing annual ratio of drama exportation. Today, a variety of genres in Korean TV dramas more and more are replaced the popularity of typical Korean dramas that obtained transnational popularity previously, like Winter Sonata and DaeJangGeum, in numerous Asian countries. (Head of International Sales in KBS Media, Interview with the author, February 8, 2008)

Korean broadcasters are both enthusiastic and concerned about the rising influence of the Korean Wave regarding Japan in the East Asian region. The Korean television industry wants to build effective professional partnerships with Japan's overall more advanced television industry. In this vein, the Korean television industry focuses more on Japan by means of TV format trades with regard to drama and on production as well as marketing partnerships. The format trade of TV dramas between the two countries has notably increased recently, so it is not unusual to see a drama of Japanese origin become a Korean remake or vice versa. For example, the Korean TV dramas *Miseang* and *Memory* were remade by Fuji TV in 2016 (Choi 2018; Joo 2016) and succeeded in garnering positive audience feedback about Korean dramas. Interestingly, these two remakes illustrate that Japanese TV broadcasters are likely to be interested in Korean dramas without much of a romance story, differing from other Asian broadcasters' preferences to typical Korean romances, when they want to remake them. In Korean television, some Japanese dramas have been remade too; the recent, *Call me Mother* was a remake of the original Japanese drama *Mother*. In the Korean remake, the drama's main storyline remained quite similar to the Japanese drama, but the major characters and situational context were changed to reflect better current Korean society. Interestingly, this Korean remake was selected for the MIPTV Asian drama contest at its 2018 convention in Cannes, France, where it was showcased to an international audience.

According to Kraidy (2005), joining forces in the course of TV drama production allows media companies to share equipment, technical staff, programming know-how, and outdoor shooting locations. Indeed, this strategy also improves financial resources, including government subsidies and tax breaks. More significantly, coproduction can decrease the risk of commercial failures to a single company, because it can distribute risks across the production process by establishing multiple partnerships with advertising firms and various entertainment companies, instead of relying on a single television station or production firm. Having a partnership for TV drama production commercially benefits the participants by providing strong local supports for the actual production process and preproduction plans for filming, such as immediate hiring of local programming staff, technical facilities, administrative support for outdoor filming at foreign locations, and the casting of local actors and actresses. The Korean television industry has taken advantage of coproductions with Japanese media and sometimes with Japanese advertising firms, as their coproduced dramas can attract more Japanese audiences when the finished drama first broadcasts in both countries. In general, it is much easier to actively run local promotion of coproduced dramas.

Some coproduced Korean dramas such as *IRIS*, *Celebrity Sweetheart*, and *Bad Man* adopted a slightly different method of a coproduction partnership with Japan. All these dramas developed a number of episodes set in different cities in Japan and actively promoted these cities while the drama was being shot and broadcast. Moreover, the main casting of these dramas considered which of Korea's best actors and actresses were preferred by Japanese viewers. In other words, coproducing a Korean drama requires adjustments to accommodate Japanese local viewers as well as local TV conditions, so the planning of the coproduction requires the effective localization of both narrative elements and promotional factors.

The drama *TaeWangSaSinGi* (*Legend* in English) was the very first Korean drama produced by the SPC system in 2007; a Japanese entertainment group invested in the drama due to the casting of Bae Yong-Joon, who played the male lead in *Winter Sonata*. The story concept, writing, casting, and filming of this drama were controlled by KJH Production, which assumed a production role, whereas the marketing firm SSD played a role in the international promotion of the drama. TSG SPC was established for the initial production of the drama, by a joint venture among KJH Production, TUBE Entertainment, a few Korean financial investment groups, NHK (a Japanese public TV station), and AVEX (a Japanese Entertainment Group). The NHK's investment of $52 million (USD) in this drama secured the exclusive presale rights of its DVD in Japan, so it invested in the TSG SPC at the beginning of production (Ministry of Culture, Sports, and Tourism 2012).

TaeWangSaSinGi was broadcast in September 2007 on MBC in Korea, where it garnered TV ratings of over 30 percent, the highest rating among the dramas being broadcast at the time. KJH Production, as the main production company, sold only the domestic broadcast rights to MBC for the first run and weekly rebroadcasts. All other drama-related copyrights belonged to KJH Production, which set a surprising precedent in Korean television. In the past, Korean networks such as MBC usually had the all-rights-reserved copyright, including broadcast licenses as well as other additional sales rights, for the broadcasted drama (Ju 2017). However, the drama by the SPC system didn't earn the expected profits from the export, partly because the response from major Asian importers (except Japan) was smaller than expected. Additionally, this first coproduced SPC production delayed the completion of the whole series by more than two years from the arranged original schedule, which greatly increased the overall production costs (Jung 2009).

Another coproduced Korean drama with a Japanese marketing company exhibited an active commercial partnership on both sides. The drama *Celebrity Sweetheart*, which was produced by Olive 9, an independent Korean production company, used a coproducing sponsorship with Dentsu, the largest Japanese advertising agency. For production of the drama, Dentsu served as a major advertising sponsor and facilitated all equipment resources for the entire drama's production, outdoor filming facilities, and local technical staff for the purpose of enhancing the drama's cinematographic quality while filming in Japan. Along with Dentsu's support and ad sponsorship, the Japanese Ministry of Travel welcomed and sped up all the administrative procedures for the filming of this drama in the Tokyo and Osaka locations. The drama was well developed, with the first four episodes using on-location film from those cities to produce the dramatic foreign scenery for the main event of the storyline.

Celebrity Sweetheart was advertised more widely in Japan than in Korea because a leading female of the drama was the Korean actress Choi Ji-Woo, who is the most popular Korean actress in Japan due to her former performance in *Winter Sonata*. When foreign advertising companies sponsor a coproduction of a Korean TV drama, the drama production needs to make an indirect advertisement for the sponsoring company and the brand. To do this in a more natural way through the entire drama, it is usual to include some scenes with product placement pertaining to the sponsor's products. In *Celebrity Sweetheart*, many products and brand symbols for Dentsu appeared in specific scenes' backgrounds or sets. The products were usually background items for specific scenes, especially those surrounding the protagonist. This indirect product advertising through television shows or movies is referred to as product placement, and it has been commonly used for most Korean TV dramas. The sponsor or coproduction partner covers part of the local promotional cost of the coproduced show, and this coproduced drama becomes an effective tool for naturally advertising the local business. In this respect, coproduction of Korean dramas is considered a win-win strategy for both sides and is shown to be a highly advanced method of broadcasting and advertising at the same time. Moreover, the partnering Asian media corporations see the Korean television industry as a worthwhile foreign media partner for the mutual growth of each media industry.

As mentioned earlier, the coproduction of Korean TV dramas with regional companies changed certain generic conventions of these dramas. Foreign location filming in Korean dramas has been customized because it is more effective in getting the audience's attention when the drama begins to broadcast. Often, a soon-to-be-released drama features a foreign location setting in the first episode to add a little exotic appeal for domestic audiences, and many Korean dramas tend to be filmed in popular travel locations like Paris,

New York, and Los Angeles. However, for more impact on the regional audience, the coproduction of Korean dramas with regional media firms presents opportunities to shoot in varying cities across East Asia. Well-known U.S. or European cities used to be preferred by Korean audiences through mediated images, but Asian cities (e.g., Beijing, Shanghai, Hong Kong, Tokyo, and Taipei) filmed in recent Korean dramas have generated new interest in Asian travel among both Korean and other Asian audiences.

The outdoor scenes in Korean dramas have also resulted in increased audience curiosity, both regarding the drama itself and the shooting locations. Foreign location scenes have brought about two main effects. First, they have enriched the visual images of the drama in accordance with the storyline, so these foreign scenes increase both the reality of the drama as well as its fantasy. Second, the outdoor scenes in neighboring Asian countries can create more intimacy for local audiences living in these locations. For instance, the Korean drama *On Air* broadcast a couple of early episodes from Taiwan's resort areas; this increased Korean viewers' interest in the location itself while providing indirect travel advertising. Similarly, *Celebrity Sweetheart* was broadcast by SBS (a Korean commercial network) but was shot in Japan, seeking to increase the allure of the drama's stylish visual images and realism while commercializing the cities of Tokyo and Osaka.

In addition, utilizing Asian locations for Korean dramas contributes to better relations with the residents in shooting locations when it is broadcast in different countries. While TV format adaptation from East Asian TV shows increases mutual content exchange, the coproduction of Korean dramas with East Asian media partners is also used to promote Korean TV dramas' commercial success in Asian television markets. In sum, as described above, the coproduction with Japanese media or entertainment firms facilitates highly advanced commercial tactics by Korean TV production companies to cater to local tastes and preferences. Of course, the Japanese entertainment industry overall is very skillful at taking advantage of the Korean drama's popularity for their own profits when conducting partnerships with Korea, even when those partnerships differ slightly from the typical focus of a drama coproduction.

Part II

TRANSNATIONAL KOREAN TELEVISION IN AMERICA

Chapter 4

Digital Audiences, Fans, and Fandom

Television has converged with various new technologies (Casey et al. 2008), so the global television industry is seriously passionate about creating new convergence cultures. Indeed, today's digital media environment facilitates an unprecedented amount of choice as well as unencumbered access, as consumers connect online to both corporate media and amateur content crossing national borders (Kustritz 2015). Moreover, several recent communication technologies focus on socializing via networking software, such as Wikis, blogs, tagging, and social networking, all of which emphasize new ways for people to interact with others (Jenkins, Ito, and boyd 2016). Television shows from different national origins have become more widespread among transnational audiences due to their advanced digital accessibility, as well as increasing migration of people beyond national territories, both online and offline.

When thinking of television audiences, one might first think of a domestic audience who consumes the majority of content from a specific national origin and only then consider international or transnational audiences who also consume foreign content produced outside their home country. Jean Chalaby (2016, 47–48) stated that transnational TV channels within Europe have multiplied and grown in diversity over the past ten years; further, they have innovated global television flows. His remark is reliable in light of multinational media corporations' geo-cultural influences on television production and distribution, especially when focusing on the relationship between the global media market and transnational audiences. Unfortunately, this does not tell us about how national differences in transferring content trigger transnational audiences to create different patterns of consumption, or about how they contribute to promoting a certain media flow across borders despite the remaining geo-cultural divisions of the mediascape.

More importantly, transnational fans or active consumers of a certain national media are not homogenous. Rather, their differences in location, sociocultural context, and political context can be much more meaningful as compared to knowing the quantity of transnational media content in the processes of reception, meaning making, involvement behaviors, community building, and fan subcultural production (Kustritz 2015). User-generated content websites, peer-to-peer networks, video streaming sites, and even social media play a central role in transnational cultural circulation (Jung 2011; Kaplan and Haenlein 2010).

No doubt, pop culture consumers are increasingly globalized and more visible through their online consumption; however, transnational television audiences are not easy to identify by conventional methods of gauging television viewership such as TV ratings. Even empirical data can often be quite ambiguous for identifying the actual viewership of the disseminated foreign TV content. Lacking a meticulous analysis of online television viewership, media scholarship has continued to iterate similar arguments and cultural assumptions about transnational television flows, typically focusing on sales of TV dramas and other serial genres. For example, Germany and England are the most important distributors of television content within the European Union, but European TV series are rarely exported outside Europe. More significantly, the presence of Asian and African countries' television content flows in transnational contexts are still restricted media landscape, thanks to global cultural barriers, at least compared to other Western television distributors (Bielby and Harrington 2008).

Henry Jenkins introduced the term *pop cosmopolitanism* to evaluate the ways that globalization influences the flow of goods, workers, financial capital, and media content from the East to the West. He noted that many teens in the East consume American popular culture to present their generational differences, while Western youth, in a similar vein, distinguish their identities by consuming various audiovisual content from the East, such as Japanese animations and Bollywood films (Jenkins 2004). Jenkins emphasizes that pop cosmopolitanism is being exponentially promoted by grassroots interests in transnational (or transcultural) circulations of pop products, and that it reasserts the bottom-up control of transnational media flows by media consumers and numerous groups of fans for certain nations' content. In the meantime, the growing impact of the grassroots in transnational media flows excel corporate media's control for transnational audiences' activities within the global pop culture market (Lee 2015). Taken all together, the ever-growing transnational or transcultural consumption of television content in global media landscapes can't be reduced to a behavioral shift based on the increasing accessibility of digital platforms (Jenkins et al. 2016). Instead, this trend has altered the dynamics of active participatory cultures by audiences, corporate media's market-driven control, and online media's transnational inclusion beyond the broadcast and cable television industry.

In this chapter, I present a case study of television audiences' online consumption of foreign TV shows, especially consumption via primary streaming platforms such as Netflix. It is worth conducting an empirical analysis of online K-drama consumption alongside streaming viewership, because the growing body of literature within online fan studies has not yet clarified who consumes the content or to what extent levels of involvement in K-drama consumption differ between viewers and fans. Unlike the online fan community, streaming platforms include wide viewer groups that can be categorized as fans, nonfans, and anti-fans[1] (see Harrington and Bielby [2005]) based on their different levels of preference for and involvement in K-drama. Methodologically, previous scholarship on K-drama's transnational viewership on Netflix (more broadly, streaming viewership) has never delved into the meanings, differences, and functionalities to assess the roles of transnational dissemination of Korean TV shows. No similar case studies have described how streaming viewership handles foreign TV consumption in transnational contexts. More importantly, the analysis in this chapter showcases the currency of Netflix viewers' specific viewing and participatory cultures as they contact emerging non-Western TV shows at the site of pop entertainment.

NETFLIX AND KOREAN DRAMA VIEWERS IN AMERICA

In the United States, Korean TV dramas are watched predominantly through streaming sites and YouTube. Based on my own interviews of American K-drama viewers (Ju and Lee 2015) and ongoing personal communications regarding both Korean TV shows and movies, a majority of U.S. interviewees use Netflix as the main channel to check out Korean TV shows. While Netflix provides a broad section of international TV shows, including East Asian TV shows and K-drama, raising cultural impact to media consumers via streaming technology, it has largely been neglected in the study of television audiences. Recently, Netflix's shift into the televisual production of original programming has sparked some media studies scholarship, but this interest is still restricted to popular titles such as *House of Cards* and *Orange is the New Black* (Burroughs 2018).

Netflix's curated collection of Korean TV shows includes trendy catalogs of K-dramas catered to geo-cultural viewers in the global platform service. Because Netflix subscriptions are managed by geographical restrictions on the accessed platform, its TV show catalogs vary by the territory where the streaming is provided. K-drama has consistently been available for the U.S.

site in the regular catalog of TV shows; more recently, Korean variety shows have been added as well. Given the increasing circulation and consumption of Korean TV shows by U.S. viewers, it is timely and important to consider their peculiar reception behaviors, emotional stances, and critical perceptions. According to Mai and King (2009), both the narratives and visual scripts of foreign TV shows are likely to be translated on the basis of the local receiving community in terms of locals' subjective experiences engaging in the conveyed events and messages. Netflix viewers' consumption of K-dramas can probe the interplay of viewers' transcultural, emotional, and behavioral engagement, both in terms of their entertainment as well as their interpretive process for cultural inclusion.

Methodologically, it is challenging to analyze Netflix viewers' actual reactions to watching K-dramas on the U.S. site because Netflix maintains subscribers' anonymity. However, there is a review board for subscribers within each K-drama page that serves as a recommendation system to all subscribers, utilizing the functions of both star ratings and the number of "helpful" comment ratings for each review. Every show can be reviewed this way and the most-viewed reviews appear at the top of the show page. Aside from star ratings and comments, the review board on Netflix offers no real-time interactive mechanisms.[2]

Despite this hurdle, substantial observations of the posted review comments justify their use as analytic data, to probe naturalized viewer engagement in streaming K-dramas. First of all, using review comments is appropriate to observe Netflix K-drama viewers' raw opinions, emotions, and moreover their tendency to engage, or not, after viewing. Second, the posted reviews for each series within a certain time frame represented mixed narratives of attitudinal, emotional, and experiential comments. Moreover, many review comments indicated that the review was posted right after (or sometimes in the middle of) watching a K-drama and certainly explore viewers' immediate feelings and opinions about the drama they've just consumed. This immediacy sets the review data apart from personal interviews with transnational K-drama fans or posts from online fan communities that were frequently adopted in earlier reception studies. Above all, my analysis of these reviews offers the opportunity to map out the mechanism of Netflix viewers' K-drama consumption as well as how similar and/or different American viewers engage with K-dramas online.

More specifically, my analysis of K-drama reviews on Netflix between February 2016 and January 2018 explores several mixed viewer groups for K-dramas, including first-time viewers, revisitors, and self-identified fans, as well as some viewers who decided not to watch any more K-dramas on Netflix after finding no relevance to the storyline. In line with levels of preference, these Netflix viewers shared their individual anecdotes and candid feelings about the dramas they watched. More often, first-time viewers called attention to their unexpected involvement in the drama and expressed their newfound attention to it by emphasizing their brand new experience, stating "This was my first Korean drama I've ever watched" or "It's the first Korean drama I've watched." Unlike the first-time viewers, self-identified fans accentuated their plentiful (or tenacious) watching experiences of K-dramas in the posted review comments and expressed, "I'm a big fan of Korean movies and TV" or "I regularly watch Korean dramas." These fans spoke of their regular and frequent exposure to K-dramas and pinpointed their longtime loyalty in accessing K-dramas. In addition, the review comments from self-identified fans not only elaborate the K-drama's narrative tactics and character development in detail, but also include critical or sharp comments on some unsatisfactory production elements, plot development, and characters' unfitness. These fans often enunciated their prolific knowledge of K-dramas to endorse themselves as K-drama fans.

Another group, revisitors, seemed to watch K-dramas less frequently than the self-identified fans, but they often shared their preferred K-drama repositories, stating that they liked to rewatch them and felt in love with the stories. Revisitors also check out new popular K-dramas for occasional entertainment. Revisitors did not hide their repetitive viewing habits at all: they insisted that rewatching their preferred K-drama was worthwhile because even if they remembered the storyline, the associated feelings were different for each viewing. According to Mittell (2015), the rewatchability of many complex TV serials has increased in the United States because viewers want to utilize their increased base of knowledge about the serial, such as moments of revelation, and because complex narratives encourage viewers to explore foreshadowing or buried information through rewatching. However, the revisitors of K-dramas on Netflix cited a different reason for rewatching the drama: they wanted to rekindle the emotional catharsis from rewatching practices, rather than recapturing the storyline.

As mentioned, the review comments on Netflix can in part fill recommendation roles for other subscribers; many of the analyzed reviewers seemed to be aware that other viewers could refer to their comments. In turn, some reviews containing critical accounts of a particular drama, beyond the viewer's own feelings and preferences, earned more "helpful" ratings. Such in-depth or critical review comments offered the viewer's personal evaluation on certain K-dramas, primarily focusing on storylines, characters, and production quality from a comparative perspective. For example, one reviewer shared, "I don't normally like or watch K-dramas of this variety, but I decided to give this one a try after reading so many positive reviews" (Review of K-drama, *You Are Beautiful* on Netflix, July 2016). In terms of this referring role, first-time viewers and revisitors left more comments related to emotional pleasures than the self-identified fans did. It is noteworthy that the self-identified fan reviewers attempt to introduce each drama based on their experiential knowledge about the typical form of Korean drama genres as well as narrative formation. They thus tended to comprehend Korean dramas' peculiar and universal characteristics in narratives, characters, cinematography, acting, and plot development on the whole. By doing so, these fan viewers tried to sharpen their reviews of certain dramas by comparing them to other American or Asian series, so U.S. viewers already familiar with the genre could understand the differences:

> Comparable with average American TV series though the depiction of a different culture adds an exotic feature. Acting is poor especially William who is inferior to average high school drama student. [. . .] Nevertheless, the series is no less entertaining than most prime time American TV programs. [3 stars, 2 helpful]
>
> (Review of K-drama, *Tamra, the Island* on Netflix, February 2016)
>
> The Japanese version of this drama is so much better. Mischievous kiss: love in Tokyo is the Japanese version of this drama. At least the guy is a little nice to her after they get married in the Japanese version. [1 star, 6 helpful]
>
> (Review of K-drama, *Playful Kiss* on Netflix, February 2016)
>
> This show rocks! I love the main actor and the female detective. Everyone seems to have secrets. This is a great mystery with good acting and dialogue. The music gets a bit dramatic but I like it. I can keep the characters straight but still cannot figure out exactly what is going on. I am on Episode 6! [. . .] It looks like the Koreans are right up there with the Nordic countries in making great mystery shows. [5 star, 3 helpful]
>
> (Review of K-drama, *Stranger* on Netflix, January 2018)

As shown in the reviews, these two Korean dramas—*Tamra, the Island* and *Playful Kiss*—have very divided evaluations among Netflix viewers, and their reviews engage in what Nancy Baym (2000) calls interpretive practice in response to the dramas' textual meanings. Likewise, some reviews expressed so much enjoyment and love for both dramas in accordance with the typical romantic and comic pleasures derived from popular Korean romance dramas. However, other reviews offered counter accounts, highlighting narratives and characters they disliked. These negative reviews usually stressed how both the male and female characters' interactions were simpleminded, which led the viewers to dislike the drama or see it as nonsensical. This contrast illustrates how television dramas are understood and received in a nation-centric framework by viewers. Reviewers on Netflix might acknowledge the differences in production and narrative forms due to a K-drama's noticed foreignness, but this difference can't be easily construed as a symbolic distinction to be interpreted or translated via embedded different cultural sensibilities.

It is significant that some exotic presentations of Korean domestic culture in the K-dramas streamed via Netflix were not well received or understood, so these Netflix viewers had a hard time making sense of specific cultural nuances and implicational notes, causing ambiguity in certain K-drama narratives. In this case, viewers find it difficult to relate more deeply with the drama, so their viewing experience ends up not being pleasurable or even confused. Several negative reviews by viewers who decided not to watch any more K-dramas on Netflix illustrated their feelings that the K-drama narratives were of no relevance. By and large, this kind of critique is taken into consideration differently for other viewers who are not yet familiar with K-dramas on Netflix. In one sense, the critique transfers cultural knowledge of Korean drama narratives to future viewers, although this seems an anti-commercial message about the drama. In another sense, the critical review opens up a certain K-drama's textual meaning for unfamiliar viewers, so they can see how much it is worth.

Despite linguistic differences and unordinary feelings for the presented narratives, transnational viewers, especially fans, tend to engage in a preferred foreign show due to the emotional relevance of the show's narrative elements, which is referred to affective affinity. Chin and Morimoto (2013) argued that affective affinity plays a large role in transcultural fandom and that it functions for transcultural consumers, especially fans, to draw attention to transcultural content, despite cultural distances, barriers, and different tastes. In this vein, affective affinity enables transnational audiences to keep seeking out the preferred transnational content in order to voluntarily refine the unique cultural sensibility conveyed by the consumed content. For K-drama reviewers on Netflix, their perceived affective affinity is at the center of the dramas' pleasure and provides a noteworthy value in its consumption. For instance, one Netflix review described the emotional function of K-dramas noted as "therapy":

> I loved all the Korean TV Dramas that I've seen on Netflix and I wished that they wouldn't take them off because when I'm done with my physical therapy these Korean TV Dramas are also a therapy to me I've rated them all a Five out of five.
>
> (Review of K-drama, *You Are Beautiful* on Netflix, February 2016)

Kim (2013) found that female K-drama viewers most often reference a certain therapeutic quality in the emotional way they talk about characters and the circumstances of the characters' lives. In the same token, the reviews on Netflix pinpointed the viewer's deep relevance in sense-making while emotionally encountering the entire story:

> This is absolutely the best "television" I've watched in years. Gripping and emotional, with twists and turns that keep you on the edge of your seat the entire time—with messages about corruption that resonate just as much here in the US as they surely must in South Korea. Stellar performances from every single cast member, with intricate yet tight writing make this a must-see. [5 stars, 4 helpful]
>
> (Review of K-drama, *Stranger* on Netflix, December 2017)

> Beautifully written, filmed, directed and acted! Will make you angry, happy, joyful and sad all at the same time. Han Ji Min, Jung Woo Sung, Kim Bum and the actress who played lead characters mom were awesome! Be sure to have tissues available because you will be on an emotional roller-coaster ride that does not stop but you don't want it to end either! I really loved this series and will definitely watch it again! [5 stars, 3 helpful]
>
> (Review of K-drama, *Padam Padam* on Netflix, February 2016)

Foreign TV shows' narratives have different styles of unfolding narratives owing to their nation-centered production convention, which may require extra effort to comprehend the plot and different narrative elements referencing certain cultural literacy. Transnational viewers in this context also need additional cultural interpretations as well as cultural translations in order to absorb the show. If transnational viewers are willing to enjoy the foreign show, this alternative way of interpreting the foreign TV narrative can be regarded as a reward and a primary pleasure that they have never experienced from their domestic TV shows (Casey et al. 2008). On Netflix, the first-time viewers' reviews expressed surprise at their instant attraction to the K-drama they watched, and often tried to explain their deep involvement in the drama based on building specific emotional reactions and attachments to characters.

It appears that Netflix viewers enjoy particular K-dramas when they see characters that enable them to reminisce about the situated main event. Through deeper involvement in K-drama narratives, some Netflix viewers try to identify themselves with one of the characters they liked; these viewers are willing to understand how and why the character behaved in certain ways presented by the drama. This in-depth understanding of the drama in association with a certain character drives viewers' parasocial interactions with a character beyond the imagined world of the drama. Indeed, the drama world is more identical to the viewer's lifeworld in their minds and viewers develop an intensive emotional connection with the characters (Kim and Wong 2012). This synchronous articulation to certain characters in K-dramas happened more often in the narratives associated with a universal and lifelike story based on the current reality. A review of the drama *Stranger* (broadcast by TVN in Korea 2018) pinpointed this aspect:

> Bravo, brava. From beginning to end. So good and yet with the current state of things you wonder if there's any government in existence not faltering under the weight of corruption. And yet . . . and yet . . . I'm still left with a sense of hope for a world where people still create better ones.
>
> (Review of K-drama, Stranger on Netflix, January 2018)

Certainly, many review postings for K-dramas on Netflix contend that the characters of each K-drama are the key element to increase keen attention and affective affinity among transnational viewers, if the characters are well woven into the drama's entire narrative. Netflix viewers are not largely conscious of distinct cultural nuances or accents that K-dramas present. For some reviewers, in particular first-time viewers and self-identified fans, cultural accents may serve as extra pleasure, and for some critical reviewers they may be disregarded and not be pertinent to their engaging in the drama when characters and their reactions seem appropriate for investing their minds and hearts.

Above all, affective affinity (Chin and Morimoto, 2013) is demonstrated as the central virtue in these Netflix viewers' consumption of K-dramas. Affective affinity primarily triggers designated transnational television consumption among all three groups of viewers: first-time viewers felt surprised by their natural affections for K-dramas, while both revisitors and self-identified fans wanted to be entertained by a broad swath of emotional experiences through different or the same kind of dramas. For Western online viewers, especially K-drama fans, this serves to draw attention to other Asian media content beyond Korean content, despite cultural distances, barriers, and different tastes. In this vein, affective affinity is the most common and critical reaction by transnational television viewers and their fan communities. Both online and offline studies examine self-voluntary involvement in preferred narratives as well as viewers' further behavioral participation in various parasocial interactions with other fans and the drama-related community.

All three types of viewers on the Netflix U.S. site shared common binge-watch practices that led them to get involved more deeply in K-dramas they preferred:

> My rear end hurts from binge watching this show for three days. My boss is mad at me too. The casting directors did a bang up job filling the roles for each of the characters. The lead actor gives a convincing performance of a man who doesn't feel emotions like normal people. The tone becomes progressively tense with each new development, which left me questioning my assumptions. Major

events aren't overdone and are woven well throughout series. I hope there's a season 2!

(Review of K-drama, *Stranger* on Netflix, December 2017)

To varying degrees, other transnational K-drama fans have pointed out similar binge-watching patterns, and indeed it seems to be a viewing ritual among K-drama viewers overseas. While some might define binge-watching as a weekend-long marathon of nonstop TV watching, the majority of online TV viewers define it as "watching between 2–6 episodes of the same TV show in one sitting" (Kelly West 2013). Netflix viewers in the United States are no exception to this trend, and it is likely that Netflix's streaming method—offering a full set of episodes for each drama—makes it easy to cultivate the ever-growing binge-watching habit (Jenner 2017; Mikos 2016).

The compact form of most K-dramas helps foster viewers' binge-watching. Unlike U.S. shows, most Korean dramas only run for one season composed of less than twenty-four episodes, forming a complete narrative arc. Many viewers can therefore finish the full show quickly, in only one or two days of seamless watching. If viewers like a couple of early episodes, it is hard for them to stop watching in the middle when there are only a few episodes left. Viewers get used to preserving the resonant mood and feelings episode by episode and then want to maintain this pace while seeking out the ending of the story. It is assumed that binge-watching may create deeper and stronger viewers' reception to these virtual and textual stories. Similarly, several Netflix viewers mentioned that they often catch up on K-dramas while binge-watching them, because they could feel more deeply about the whole narrative than if they had watched it one or two episodes at a time. Jenner (2017) asserted that TV viewers' binge-watching illustrates an intersection of discourses on industry, audience, and texts surrounding the complex contemporary TV landscape. When binge-watching a TV series, viewers also integrate their personal lives and minds into fictional narratives more deeply (Mikos 2016).

Although the anonymity on Netflix members' review boards restricts revealing the viewers' cultural and ethnic identities—this is not only the case for Netflix but for many recent online fan communities in transnational media—some reviewers on Netflix highlighted their Korean drama preference as being not closely tied to their own ethnic identities.

> Just finished watching this show and it was great! It left me so emotionally drained and dehydrated from crying so much! But it does have many cute and funny moments. [. . .] I had not seen any Korean dramas before as I'm Mexican American and usually watch telenovelas or soaps, but these two shows got me

hooked. I will be watching Secret Garden next. Thanks for having these programs in your lineup. [5 stars, 5 helpful]

(Review of K-drama, *Moon Embracing the Sun* on Netflix, February 2016)

Just so you know, I am a white 56-year-old woman. I LOVED this show! It is as good or better than most American crime dramas/mysteries. Great acting, exciting, and suspenseful plot, and satisfying end. I enjoy hearing another language and getting arm-chair travel by watching foreign shows. If, however, you have trouble reading fast-paced subtitles, this may be challenging for you. Occasionally I had to pause to catch up in the dialogue. I tried to watch another Korean drama, and the music was way too sappy, and the acting very melodramatic. This show does not feel like that and had some good humor as well. [5 stars, 5 helpful]

(Review of K-drama, *Stranger* on Netflix, December 2017)

It is noteworthy that these viewers' preferences for a particular Korean drama stem from different narratives and ways of presenting characters than those found in similar genres of American TV shows. Moreover, these viewers seek out dramatic narratives featuring central and appealing Asian casts, which is quite unusual in American TV shows. Indeed, Asians in American television have been cast in marginal roles and moreover depicted as quite homogenous and stereotypical, evidencing racial approaches primarily relying on a White American perspective. In contrast to the American television perspective, K-dramas provide charming and active Asian characters beyond the typified racial and ethnic stereotypes, which may be the most refreshing aspect that K-dramas can give Western viewers who are seeking foreign shows.

According to Schulze (2013), transnational K-drama fans' activities emphasize discussions about the storyline of the drama, its plot development, possible endings, the motivations of protagonists, realistic depiction of characters, episode summaries, and predictions for future episodes. Through these activities, fans attempt to interpret the layers of the Korean drama texts as accurately as possible from their own cultural standpoints, not from the standpoint of Korea's own culture and society. Schulze (2013, 376–377) refers to this as an "ethnohermeneutic" reading and notes that international fans of Korean television create some general rules or popular narratives from K-dramas as an ordinary fan activity; they use these rules or tropes to share their own creative story world conveyed by Korean dramas and to increase a collective sense of the drama's unique symbolic meanings while decoding the contained meanings. Some Netflix viewers' articulations of their own ethnic identities in Korean drama reviews may relate to their desire to share their own ethnohermeneutic readings of the drama with the broader viewer community. It certainly underscores the capacity of different narrative formulations, production styles, and characters in Korean dramas to create a more intimate appeal to multiethnic viewers who are seeking a new pop culture resource.

VIEWERS, FANS, AND FAN STUDIES ON TRANSNATIONAL TELEVISION

In critical cultural studies, audience reception research on both domestic and transnational television shows offers us delicate insights into viewers' behavioral tendencies, interpretive, and semiotic meaning-making practices in tandem with the viewers' local identities. As Grossberg (1992) argued, the production-end analysis and political economy approaches in media studies present only the state of media texts before they reach the audience in a particular media environment. This line of research therefore does little to probe exactly what difference the audience makes with media texts. On the contrary, reception research on a particular TV show or film has contributed to our knowledge of televisual narratives and its elements and how they most influence the audience in terms of subjectivity and culture. In this vein, reception research sheds light on the various ways audiences engage with specific media texts and how to define media audience as a sociocultural community, instead of as an economic segment of media consumers.

Before digital media converged to television, few media scholars had discussed how television audiences engage in content production (and not merely content reception) because audiences' activities were involved in the reproduction of secondary texts of the received content, seeking their own meanings and sources of the pleasure from certain television content as audiovisual texts (see Fisk 1989; Morley 1992; de Certeau 1984; du Gay 1997). Here, what they called "audience" actually indicated the common characteristics of fans for television shows. As they argued, television audiences who conduct further discursive practices beyond their viewing experience of a TV show tend to be fans of that show. In other words, media fans can be defined as a set of audience members who feel an intense emotional connection to a particular media text and participate in discursive as well as participatory practices, to cultivate additional pleasures and collective interactions regarding the preferred media text. In line with this definition, a body of in-depth reception research on television texts has been regarded as a form of fan studies.

To a certain extent, fan studies in academia has frequently been criticized for examining fundamentally female-centric, irrational, excessively emotional, and impulsive practices of media audiences, who usually comprise a small number of members associated with particular programs. The terms *fan* or *fandom* have often been used pejoratively, mostly to describe those who are entertained by their preferred media genres, such as soap operas, romances, fantasies, or pop music (Gray 2003). This assumption might work well in the domestic television context, but in a transnational context it is considerably narrower, focused on the differentiation between fans and general viewers. Based on the Western media fandom literature, television fandom is a form of subculture in which some avid viewers can create alternative entertaining spaces for themselves away from mainstream media, so these fans are eager to devote themselves to certain fan activities (Otmazgin and Lyan 2013). In particular, Western media fandom plays an often overlooked role in spreading new transnational cultures, such as East Asian media culture. For instance, earlier fans of Japanese animation and manga were marked as nerdy cultural maniacs and their activities were conceived to be a result of Orientalist world fantasies. But today, it is essential that media fandom researchers be closely attuned to the sociocultural complexity of transnational media flows as well as fans' mobilization across borders via online media platforms.

Television shows increasingly cross national borders and are disseminated to diverse foreign locations, mainly due to increasing online transmission as well as widespread international fandoms. In this increasing online consumption of transnational TV shows, Paul Booth's approach (2010) to digital fandom studies offers important insights. According to Booth (2010, 39), "Fans both influence and are influenced by technology not just as tools, but also as necessary and catalytic mechanisms to alter their subjective experiences of cultural life. Fans use digital technology not only to create, to change, to appropriate, to poach, or write, but also to share, to experience together, to become alive with community."

Booth also noticed that even under digital media environments, fandom hasn't changed as much from its original roles as media scholarship implicitly indicates. Online practices influence but do not monopolize conventional fan practices overall, and in turn TV fandom especially integrates online communal activities into offline practices at the same time. Offline fan practices still strengthen individual fans' identification with a certain show (or character) and online fan communities establish individual fans' bonds as the part of a larger group, regardless of their differences in nationality, language, gender, and sexuality. In addition, online fandom for TV shows provides a comfort zone for individual fans not apart from their imagined narrative world, enabling immediate interactions with companions sharing their interest in media and pop culture.

Online fandom, particularly for television shows, builds creative textual spaces where fans play with the show, imagining new textual and graphical components of their preferred shows. For example, fans creatively remix videos of main characters, write free subtitles in local languages for foreign TV shows, recapture videos for particular episodes, and remix official trailers. Online fandom for television dramas organizes few activities as formal communal behaviors but centralizes individual fans' parasocial practices in regard to preferred episodes or characters in the discussed drama. They often share photographs of a particular scene and post regular updates on different cast members. Through online fan communities, television fans want to be involved in the narratives of the show itself. In many cases, fans like to change original narratives to take another direction; many television shows' endings instigate fan discussions and fans get involved in making alternative endings or different climaxes of the show, responding to other fans. Recently, one prevalent example of fans' articulation of narratives involves the action of transmitting spoilers of TV dramas. Spoilers provide fans' or viewers' assumed synopsis with regard to what is to come in the next episodes or even what happens in the ending of the drama (Mittell 2015).

Using spoilers, online fan communities can increase energetic discursive communications not only among fan members but also between viewers and fans. Spoilers, whether intentional or not, are effective commercial messages to promote the show and some avid fans are likely to share spoilers for the sake of broadly promoting a show in some cases. Through such parasocial activities and networking in online fan communities, individual fans grow their intimacy toward the entire fan community but also deepen their knowledge of the specific mediated drama amid complex interactions online (Booth and Kelly 2013). Again, in this digital environment, television fandom parallels both online and offline interactions and the two modes of fandom influence one another. Online fandom tends to generate interactive dialogues without many barriers between fan members or fans and viewers; offline fandom still illustrates deep interactions between individual fans that recall their collective fan identity by means of actual performances, such as local meet-ups, drama-related events, and annual pop convention meetings (Booth and Kelly 2013). Online fandom, including Korean drama fandom, recognizes the potential of transnational television fan communities and changes the ways in which international fans get involved in foreign TV series.

Netflix viewers on the U.S. site, as examined earlier, did not perceive the authentic Korean culture from the dramas they watched; rather, the Korean culture was received as an imagined and negotiated concept through the drama's semiotic signifiers. Moving images, narrative themes, and textual meanings are decoded on the whole when these Western viewers engaged in drama worlds mainly presenting the specific sociocultural space and time of Korea. Thus, Western viewers could see the partial cultural aspects of the preferred drama and this made them feel superficial in identifying the real sense of Koreanness. For example, in chapter 2, I explained the ways romantic relationships between male and female characters are commonly developed in Korean romance dramas. The specific nonverbal gestures and manners (e.g., forms of eye contact, intimate distance, and skinships) shown in the episodes are sometimes seen as eye-opening events as well as culturally unique scenes by Western audiences. Western viewers not only observe cultural differences in Korean dramas but also attempt to find places to relate sympathetically to a given dramatic narrative. In this sense, many transnational viewers of Korean dramas watch those shows from a non-culturalist point of view (Schulze 2013). This tendency is reflected in the fact that Korean drama fans understand the drama's message or fictional features as a partial image of Koreans and Korean society. Transnational Korean drama fans take it for granted that the perceived drama world presents only a symbolic creation of Korea and Koreans, which includes a mixture of real and non-real aspects of Korea.

It is clear that the cultural perception of Korean dramas by Western viewers (or even fans) is not foregrounded. More importantly, though, Korean dramas facilitate a typical narrative of their own, revealing Korea's sensibility as images of the nation that Western viewers would like to engage through their own emotions and cultural translations. Meanwhile, these specific narratives are also intriguing and entertaining as a fresh source of pleasure. Notably, online fan websites of Korean dramas contribute to building these enthusiastic viewers' collective activities and their negotiated interpretive practices across borders, to make more sense of many different aspects of Korean dramas. Today, the primary streaming TV services, such as Netflix, contribute to broadening the spectrum of Korean drama's transnational viewers.

NOTES

1. Harrington and Bielby (2005, 908) borrowed and slightly altered Gray's (2003) terminology about the kinds of viewers in the context of global television, to explain the viewers' different capacity for consumption of transnational media content. According to them, the target audience in foreign TV show markets today may be composed of three potential groups: fans, nonfans, and anti-fans. Fans are attracted to cultural texts preceding the act of consumption. In describing anti-fans, they use Gray's definition that these viewers are not necessarily those who are against fandom per se, but those who strongly dislike a given text or genre for many reasons or no reason. Finally, nonfans are referred to "those viewers or readers who do view or read a text, but not with any intense involvement" (Gray 2003, 74). Here, the concept of

nonfans might also include nonviewers who did not enact any previous consumption, although nonfans and nonviewers are not interchangeable.

2. The author observed and collected the posted K-drama review comments from a review board for subscribers within each K-drama page on U.S. Netflix site between February 2016 and January 2018. In the middle of 2018, Netflix changed the streaming service design of "K-dramas" and since then a review board for subscribers has not offered through the entire K-drama catalog.

Chapter 5

The Power of Streaming TV
Netflix, DramaFever, and American Viewers

In the early 2000s, the emergence of digital media sounded a note of woe for the shrinking role of television. But since then, television and the Internet have solidified the most successful case of synergy in media convergence, as they both activate and broaden television audiences to create a more participatory TV culture (Nikunen 2007) that crosses borders. For years, YouTube has been the preferred video platform, allowing many people around the world to share and distribute various kinds of audiovisual content. Its video-sharing technology, such as user-generated videos, contributes to individuals reproducing their favorite TV shows into self-edited fan-subbing videos, and makes them easy to share with others (Thornton 2010).

More importantly, the rapid growth of YouTube triggered a radical shift in transnational television flows: more TV viewers of foreign TV shows access them predominantly through the Web instead of along with the scheduled TV broadcasting. This new trend associated with the digital media platforms fundamentally transformed television programming, ways of content distribution, and the method of audience viewership, changing the way general audiences engage with television (McDonald and Smith-Rowsey 2016). Jin (2017, 3880) demonstrated that social networking sites, user-generated content platforms, and search engines have become the new outlets of the media and popular culture, and that global fans become more capable of consuming popular culture forms from other countries by increasing their choices of digital media platforms.

In the meantime, the rise of global content providers within popular culture, including streaming video services such as Netflix, Amazon Prime, and Hulu, greatly influences transnational television flows in multiple dimensions, such that the diversity of international TV and film not only flows out of the United States, but also increasingly different national content flows into the United States (Chung 2011). Thanks to the surge in streaming video services, East Asian TV shows have an increased chance to be introduced on U.S. media outlets (Molen 2014) in tandem with legally licensed content, and Korean TV shows frequently appear to American viewers who previously had little exposure to non-Western TV programs.

Given the noticeable impact of streaming platforms on K-dramas' penetration into the United States, in this chapter, I examine streaming platforms for Korean TV drama in the United States, discuss how streaming K-dramas cater to viewers in the United States, where foreign TV shows often struggle to capture a domestic audience, and consider in what ways streaming TV platforms in the United States help motivate a new order of transnational television flows to U.S. audiences as one segment of Western audiences. More than ever, Korean TV shows have tangible inflows to North America and Europe, but global media scholarship has done little to investigate this new pattern of increasing non-Western media players, their general audience engagement, and their consumption amongst U.S. and other Western audiences. A few studies have examined how K-pop (transnational Korean pop music) penetrates the West, for example, BTS syndrome, and how it influences youth culture (e.g., Fuhr 2015; Hong-Mercier 2013; Yoon 2017). Still, there is a need to keenly explain and demonstrate the nature of Korean television flows into the U.S. media, including networks, cable, and streaming websites. Certainly, U.S. television has dominated the global television markets and international audiences, with their domestic programs forming the global center of soft power, so the broadened consumption (or reception) of K-dramas via streaming platforms by U.S. audiences is an evolving trend that calls for more attention. This line of research should consider both a theoretical typology between Western countries and non-Western countries and establish methodologies for more rigorous analyses of the burgeoning online TV viewership of non-Western TV shows, including streaming TV, by U.S. audiences.

DIVERGENT TRANSNATIONAL TV CONSUMPTION IN THE AGE OF MEDIA CONVERGENCE

Over the years, the central analyses of transnational television flows on a global scale have tended to emphasize the strength of Western programs' penetration to different territorial regions, especially since the U.S.- and European-produced content relies on mainstream media trade circuits (Chalaby 2010, 2016a; Harrington and Bielby 2005; Haven 2006). Generally it is difficult to notice the meager flows of non-Western TV programs toward Western countries and the linked viewership, due to their meager commercial impacts in the global mediascape. By this token, the political economy of the global media flows has been oversimplified as a typology of transnational media across the world, centering on large streams of the major Western countries' media and content. As a result, a number of small nations' or regions' border-crossing media flows with limited audience groups have been overlooked, along with a long economic imbalance of cultural power between the East and West.

While the political economy of global media flows still works on a macro level of analysis, things have been enormously changed by the advent of media convergence on a micro level of analysis, which extensively reshaped and continues to stimulate different TV viewing patterns and engagement practices in many parts of the world. The converging media culture with digital platforms has initiated TV viewers' parallel use of the Internet and television. For instance, over 140 million Americans—55 percent of the U.S. Internet population—watch TV online (Guitton 2015) and Netflix was named the most-used streaming site (Goldhill 2014; Guitton 2015). Nowadays, Netflix's streaming service is seen as an innovation of television and more broadly of the media content business: it excels at increasing the diversity of TV and movie content online by acquiring many TV shows and movies originating outside of North America.

Looking closer into television content, it is more likely to diversify, thanks to streaming TV technologies and increasing digital platforms; the reverse flow of transnational TV content from small to large TV markets is growing simultaneously with global TV markets. This partly occurs due to the shift in the television industry from broadcasting to on-demand services, which caters to new and web-focused niche audience markets (Bielby and Harrington 2008; Lobato 2018; Yu 2013). However, it has also appeared to construct a fresh TV genre in promoting television exports by non-active or small national and regional content distributors. Havens (2006) pointed out that several nations established key TV genres to win competitions in the international TV trade, taking advantage of the established popularity of a certain TV brand. As such, Brazil has a reputation for telenovelas,[1] Germany is known for action-adventure, and Scandinavia is heralded for its reality shows.

Indeed, the inflow of K-dramas to the United States can be understood as part of the national TV brand from the Korean television industry, which seeks to expand the surging reputation of K-dramas across Asia under the Korean Wave. The current entry of K-dramas into American online television sheds light on the increasing complexity of transnational television flows, both in theoretical and industrial spectrums, that certainly challenge the given hierarchical marketability in the conventional TV show trades. Given this understanding, the growing streaming television platforms and markets around the world call for a diverse set of transnational TV shows to bolster the alternative marketability (or salability) of less popular and familiar TV genres (Ju 2019).

Alongside the converging TV environment, television viewers also voluntarily interact online with TV shows or preferred genres, regardless of the shows' production origins. This increases television producers' and marketers' attention to their programming decisions, as they are keen to grasp an emerging segment of transnational TV viewership via multiple online platforms. Although a lack of content knowledge makes transnational TV shows seem unfamiliar to many foreign viewers, these viewers' attitudes and the way they watch—or, more precisely, the way in which they are seen to watch—can make a difference in enjoying transnational TV shows (Andrejevic 2008). For instance, transnational fans of K-dramas today are enthusiastic to create multiple online fan communities through social networking sites, because they want to share their knowledge about and affection for dramas they've been watching, and moreover these fans generate different local language translations of the preferred K-dramas to share with other members, regardless of nationality (Lee 2015).

A rising number of Korean and other East Asian TV series reach overseas viewers in the same way (Lee 2011), that is, online self-entertainment efforts among TV viewers. This activity is seen not only by fans of a certain type of TV show but also by nonfan viewers looking for fresh content. In this sense, transnational TV fandom emerges primarily with the mobility of media and cultural products crossing national borders (Han 2017). Whether through fan-based online community or streaming sites, the construction of TV fandom pertinent to a national media content can be a catalyst to trigger a channel of circulation for implanting new foreign TV products in new audience markets, thus carving out transnational media industries (Otmazgin and Lyan 2013). In other words, cultural consumers' desire in this digital age increasingly transgresses temporal, spatial, and linguistic constraints, while their seamless use of online and digital platforms is intensified by their access to collective knowledge about different types of cultural products. Thus, the transnational TV viewership focusing on online practices certainly increases the complexity and disjuncture of transnational media studies when mapping them out to a constructive audience- and industry-driven mechanism. Along these theoretical lines, the next section outlines and investigates how the transnational flow of K-dramas, especially in the United States and mainly via streaming TV platforms, affects audience viewership, streaming strategies, and the cultural influences of non-Western origin content.

STREAMING KOREAN TELEVISION AND THE MEANING OF STREAMING VIEWERSHIP

In U.S. television, Asian TV shows started to tap into Asian-American audiences in the mid-2000s via traditional broadcast corporations and the development of cable networks; these channels focused on running popular TV dramas, documentaries, music, and films from mostly East Asian television. Of these, the first and foremost cable channel was AZN Television, a subsidiary of Comcast that promoted itself as the network for Asian Americans. However, AZN TV struggled and decided to shut down quickly in April of 2008, after just over a year on the air. Comcast announced the reason for this closure as difficulty generating advertising revenue (Becker 2008). Before Netflix, foreign TV shows in the United States were rarely broadcast on the mainstream TV circuit (e.g., networks and cable); they were understood as TV shows whose aim was to reach a niche audience—say, first-generation immigrants in the United States who missed their home country's TV offerings. It is worth noting that TV drama imports from Asian countries in the United States have been sought by cable systems aiming for diverse ethnic viewers, prior to legal or illegal on-demand forms. However, this was not the case with Korean television content before the rise of Korean Wave 2.0 (or Hallyu 2.0).

K-dramas first entered the U.S. television market relatively late compared to other popular foreign TV shows, such as UK drama series or telenovela, so K-dramas have a relatively low profile among U.S. viewers. While Asian viewers' large volume of Korean drama consumption has been frequently discussed, Korean drama consumption and viewership by American viewers has not. The body of literature on the overall Korean pop culture consumption by Western consumers has pinned down that K-dramas, along with K-pop, are the key consumed content among interviewed audiences (Hübinette 2012; Ju and Lee 2015; M. Oh 2014; Park 2013; Yoon 2017), despite more frequent K-pop centered discussion.

Because of the slightly different timeline when the popular K-dramas made their first appearance on the major streaming TV sites, these platforms became important distributors of Korean television content for many years, conveying mostly dramas and variety shows to Western markets. Since 2011, the big names in online streaming in the United States—Netflix, DramaFever, and Hulu—have initiated the famous K-dramas for streaming, while other license aggregators of Asian TV shows became the major distributors of K-dramas (as well as K-movie and K-pop) as part of their archived international content. In 2012, Netflix had more than 130 partners that fed its international video lineup (Yu 2013). Greg Peters, Netflix's chief streaming and partnerships officer, recently said in a media interview that Netflix likes to work with Korean television broadcasters or other market players in Korea to produce Korean content (Lee and Kim 2016).

In a chronological review, Korean-language television in the United States did not quite present in the mainstream media scene, but always seemed to be a part of diasporic broadcast channels that entertained a small number of Korean American community members, mainly located in large cities. Back in 1983, the Korean community in the United States embraced a full-fledged Korean-language TV station via the U.S. cable system. It was operated by the Korean government-owned Korean Television Enterprise (KTE) and was only available to subscribers in Los Angeles. KBS in Korea, a state-public broadcaster, managed KTE's U.S. operation, which included distributing U.S. TV shows to Korea as well as distribution of KBS-produced shows to the United States (Lee 2015). Due to the limited broadcast scope by geography as well as Korean language barriers, Korean diasporic communities across the United States became the dominant audience and most saliently consumed Korean media content—mostly TV shows, movies, and comic books—via video rental services in Korean-product retail stores available in major metropolitan cities. Until the late 1990s, the stabilized Korean diaspora TV stations and Korea-town video rental services were well established in the United States, and these two methods have long been utilized by Korean TV show consumers, who seem to be mostly ethnically Korean or other Asians.

Since the mid-2000s, the reputation of K-dramas has been captured by the major press in America and the United Kingdom (e.g., *The New York Times*, *Guardian*, *CNN*, and *BBC World*), thanks to the Korean Wave across Asia. These well-known Western news media introduced huge Asian demand for K-dramas with surprise and curiosity, and they drew more attention to why this phenomenal pop culture movement moved from Korea to all over Asia. The resulting attention to the Korean Wave naturally encouraged the general American audience to take a new look at K-dramas and other Korean pop culture, and enthusiastic audiences—the early adopters of K-dramas and K-movies—become more active in seeking out the K-dramas, films, and K-pop they'd heard about on the news.

However, these U.S. fans of K-dramas faced a lack of resources and often experienced difficulty in searching or regularly accessing full episodes of the K-dramas due to copyright restriction in the United States. At first, these U.S. fans and active audiences mainly accessed Korean pop culture content using YouTube and the well-known fan-based websites, such as mysoju.com, Viki.com, DramaCrazy.net, and allkpop.com (Ju and Lee 2015; Lee 2015; M. Oh 2014). These fan-based websites predominantly operated through file-sharing technology to distribute particular TV shows in a timely manner. They also connected K-drama viewers around the world online. Then, a large number of K-drama videos appeared which were partly edited from the original episodes, sometimes including edited audio with different voice actors. These fan-edited videos were illegal without copyright licenses from the original production house in Korea, but they have long been accessible on temporary hosts to avoid copyright infringement on the Internet portal and search engines. For entertainment purposes, the content was often reproduced in a variety of forms through editing as well as by adding completely new fabrications to the original TV show. Based on this account, the Korean Wave fan websites can be said to play a central role in widening the range of transnational audiences for K-dramas and even paved the way for legal and reliable streaming services. In addition, some fan-based websites (DramaFever.com and Viki.com are good examples), due to their huge popularity amongst transnational fans of K-dramas, have switched to being subsidies of the U.S. media corporations as streaming viewership for K-dramas and films grows.

As mentioned earlier, the Korean Wave phenomenon has shown the complexity of global media in both political economy and critical media theories, so this trend can't be simply explained by a single media mechanism. Accordingly, the overall tendency of K-drama online viewership in the United States calls for a micro level of analysis of the audience and market environment, alongside the media transformation that interconnects media industries into certain types of TV content for production, distribution, and consumption. By and large, both fan-based online communities for K-dramas (and more broadly, for Korean pop culture content) and legal and large streaming platforms are the crucial promoters of Korean television shows in the Western media market, including American television.

Previous studies on the growing subscription-based video-on-demand (SVOD) services on a global scale, especially those on Netflix, importantly confirmed that analyzing SVOD programming requires the same level of attention previously applied to the mainstream broadcast programming in global television flows (Chalaby 2016a, 2018; Lobato 2018; McDonald and Smith-Rowsy 2016). In some television markets around the world, such as Canada, the United Kingdom, Australia, New Zealand, and parts of Western Europe, Netflix provides the mainstream media as well, replacing networks and cable television in terms of consumption numbers (Lobato 2018, 243). International fans of K-dramas have repeatedly stated that they prefer to watch K-dramas online instead of through national or regional television broadcasts (Schulze 2013). Korean TV viewers in transnational contexts thus tend to gain intermediary accessibility to seek and watch K-dramas by means of digital platforms in their regions.

During the early 2000s, media scholars conducted a few audience studies about different Asian viewers of K-dramas, to test the assumption that cultural proximity[2] explains K-dramas' central appeals to Asian fans because of a shared sense of Asian identity (Mori 2008; Yang 2003; Yoo and Lee 2001). They concluded that Asian fans enjoyed a cultural affinity with K-dramas by identifying with Korean ways of life, values, physical appearance, and love relationships (Iwabuchi, 2008; Kim, 2013; Lee and Ju, 2010). To some degree, cultural proximity was later adopted to explain many young Asians' love of K-drama and/or K-pop stars and to broaden the concept to explore ethnic perceptions of Asian masculinity and femininity (Jung, 2009; Jung, 2011; Oh, 2014; Yang, 2008). Previous audience studies in this token tended to frame transnational K-drama consumption within an inter-Asian cultural context, concerned primarily with postcolonial sensibilities across modernized Asian communities (Cho, 2011; Iwabuchi, 2008; Lie, 2012).

Indeed, cultural proximity can partly explain K-dramas' success in Asia, but it tells us little about the constant spread of K-dramas in Western countries or through global streaming sites. More significantly, cultural proximity underestimates the overall transnational mobility of Korean pop culture as a cyclic iteration of one part of East Asian culture within the region (Ju 2017), so this approach has generalized the nature of the Korean Wave in a limited scope. In addition, a cultural proximity approach can neither explain the latest flow of K-drama to the United States, Canada, Latin America, and many parts of Europe, nor can it offer answers about Asian fans' consumption of popular Western TV shows alongside K-dramas (Jin, 2016). Schulze's critique of the cultural proximity approach, which filled research gap about the risks of cultural proximity studies on the Korean Wave, is a good starting point. Schulze (2013) argued that the cultural proximity model relies on a specific conceptualization of culture that is narrowly defined as a national belonging bounded only by a sovereign territory, making individual cultures discrete, tangible, bounded, stable, and enduring entities (see, e.g., Beck 2003 [2000]; Gupta and Ferguson 1999; Latour 2005). From this point of view, transnational cultural flows occur very rarely, if ever.

To extend Schulze's remarks, only a few researchers since 2012 (e.g., Correra 2012; Hong-Mercier 2013; Lee et al. 2014) have seriously delved into Internet consumption as the main medium for accessing K-dramas (Schulze 2013). Indeed, streaming of Korean TV shows is an increasingly popular method by which Western audiences enjoy a variety of Korean television content. This suggests the importance of online streaming viewership of K-dramas, as well as several variety shows, to advance the existing empirical methods in media reception and fan studies about K-dramas across different Western audiences. Recent Internet-centered studies of K-drama consumption have found that the mode of watching K-dramas on the Web creates active discussions, interactions, and diverse textual interpretations of dramatic narratives, cultural traits, and Korea itself. This active viewership may be conceptualized as a small fan community with its own cultural repertoire that prompts broader reflection on the cultural inclusion of behaviors, interactions, institutions, or objects among fans (Hong-Mercier 2013; Lee et al. 2014; Schulze 2013). In this context, we can ask whether transnational viewers of Korean TV shows differ in their consumption behaviors and affective engagement depending on their national belongings—especially in terms of Asian vs. Western viewers. In addition, the analysis of K-drama viewership on streaming platforms can contribute to probing both universal and particular modes of transnational audience consumption.

Netflix and DramaFever have been identified as the major streaming services accessed by the U.S. viewers of Korean TV shows in previous research (e.g., Lee 2015; M. Oh 2014) and in my personal interviews with Asian American viewers in 2011 (Ju and Lee 2015). For a more practical understanding about the role of streaming in the Korean TV flows, the following sections outline these two legitimate streaming platforms in the United States to better contextualize the broadened diffusion of Korean TV shows and their dedicated viewership.

NETFLIX: K-DRAMAS' GLOBAL STREAMING CHANNEL

While pay TV subscriptions in the United States rapidly declined during the past few years, the so-called Over-the-Top (OTT) services, such as Netflix and Amazon Prime Video, took their place as quickly as possible. The fastest growing OTT services are part of on-demand video services, which encompass all types of digital platforms via instant streaming online (Chalaby 2016a). In the United States, undoubtedly, Netflix is the top streaming provider in the converging media industry and even alters its members' television watching patterns in dynamic ways that promote binge watching and avoidance of advertising (Tryon 2015), by means of customizing personal content repositories. Over the past fifteen years, Netflix has achieved innovation in global content distribution online, and as a result, its size and dominance in the market have challenged the traditional forms of the entertainment industry (Novak 2016).

Netflix began online streaming of TV programs and movies in 2007 for U.S. subscribers and introduced streaming as a convenient and personalized media entertaining method. Netflix streaming technology has incorporated new algorithms that make recommendations through a personalized user interface, which in turn makes it possible to accumulate metadata on subscribers' preferences through individuals' content choices. Netflix applies this data to measure audience engagement in ways that form an abstract of their behaviors to minimize uncertainty about users' personalized practices (McDonald and Smith-Rowsey 2016).

Since the initiation of the U.S. streaming service, Netflix continues to broaden its offerings, not only in a wide range of media platforms (Elkawy et al. 2015) but also in the global operation of the service (Lobato 2018). The number of reported Netflix subscribers continues to grow: in 2013, Netflix claimed 37 million subscribers from 40 countries, as well as 35.7 million

U.S. subscribers by the end of 2014 (Goldhill 2014). Most recently, Netflix officially introduced its company in terms of global outreach: "Netflix is the world's leading internet entertainment service with 125 million memberships in over 190 countries enjoying TV series, documentaries and feature films across a wide variety of genres and languages" (Netflix.com 2018). In turn, Netflix aggressively stepped up global operations of the platform and service packages in 2010, to complement the success of their original TV series on their international platforms. Starting in the United States, the company expanded its streaming services to Canada, then to South America, Western Europe, and East and South Asia, launching in South Korea at the end of 2016. Despite Netflix's Asian service operations, China remains a complicated market that hasn't made a deal to launch the service for several years (Lobato 2018).

As a global content provider, Netflix subscriptions are managed by geographic location: members registered in the United States, for example, only have access to TV shows lined up for the U.S. site. In other words, Netflix TV show catalogs vary by the territory where the streaming is provided. Netflix's program catalogs offer filtered TV and movie content based on streaming licenses from networks, independent production corporations, and third-party producers from many different countries. In 2011, Netflix started to invest heavy in original content production, including the popular series *House of Cards* (2013), and this activated a fast-growing proportion of Netflix originals vs. licensed content. However, Netflix originals still account for less than a quarter of the overall catalog in most territories they serve, so it relies considerably on licensed content (Lobato 2018). Alongside the Netflix original series, their voluminous international TV programs keep up with the growing global operations in different territories. Given this context, transnational Korean TV shows in America call for a more detailed examination of the U.S. audience that consumes Korean TV shows via Netflix, because Korean TV shows are newer to Netflix compared to other international offerings such as British- or Spanish-language programs.

Korean TV shows were first offered to U.S. members in 2012 as one of the foreign TV show packages, while "Korean TV" has its own category in the main "TV Shows" catalog, separate from Korean movies. Netflix U.S. provides a diverse set of movies from Asia (e.g., China, Japan, and India), Latin America, and Europe (e.g., Spain, Germany, Scandinavia, France, and Italy), but as of 2017, its international TV catalog included only British-, Korean-, and Spanish-language TV shows (Ju 2019). Netflix's lineup of Korean TV shows indicates that Netflix is aware of the influence of the K-drama in the Korean Wave, as well as the commercial value of distributing transnational K-dramas through their global platforms (see figure 5.1).

In fact, in 2017 Netflix announced plans for more in-depth partnerships with Korean television and production system to produce Netflix's Korean

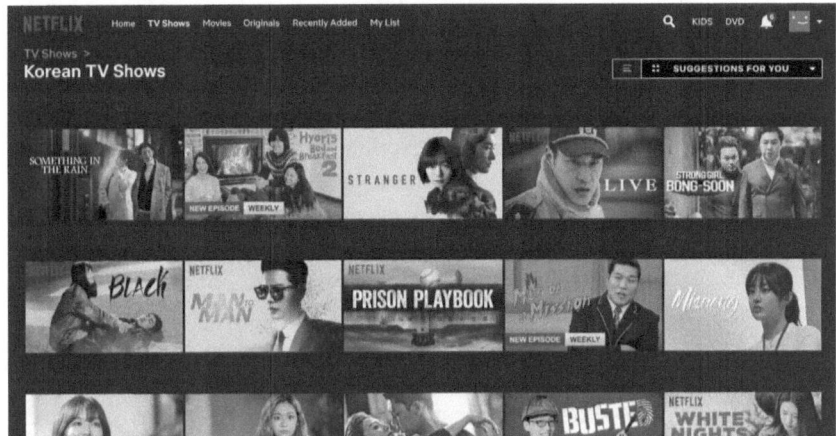

Figure 5.1 Netflix's Korean TV Shows. *Source*: Screenshot by the author.

original TV series (Herreria 2017; Kil 2017; Netflix Media Center 2017; Tan 2017) as part of its internationalization. In addition, this partnership reflects a hope for more Korean TV content and other fresh East Asian content. Netflix later clarified that its first original Korean drama production would adapt the popular Korean web comic, *Love Alarm*, in a twelve-episode drama series (Herreria 2017; Tan 2017). A few months later, Netflix released its second production lineup for a six-episode original Korean drama series called *Kingdom*. *Kingdom* was produced by a Korean production company called "A Story," funded by Netflix, while the original script was written by the well-known K-drama writer Kim Eun-hee[3] (Netflix.com 2017; Yoon 2018). *Kingdom* is the first Korean original drama to stream exclusively on Netflix's global platforms: six episodes aired in 2018, and shortly afterwards plans for another season were announced.

As seen earlier, K-dramas on Netflix are served in different service venues, which include full episodes, a brief summary of each show, and a preview of the casting. Interestingly, until 2017 the Korean TV show page offered an official review board featuring individual members' review comments on that show. Through this review board, Netflix members could rate each K-drama using a five-star system and leave their opinions or comments on the show at the same time. Although the review board offered no interactive mechanisms among reviewers in real time, it played a role in the recommendation system for other viewers if they wanted to learn more about a show in the catalog. However, Netflix changed this service venue in the middle of 2018, so the show-specific member review boards no longer exist.

Netflix has streamed the majority of K-dramas capable of streaming all the full episodes in each season, so viewers can catch up on all episodes at once;

however, some variations have appeared recently on the Netflix Korean TV show catalog, which has some dramas marked as "Netflix Original." As a consequence of the extended partnerships between Netflix and the Korean broadcasting industry mentioned earlier, some newly retrieved K-dramas have different streaming schedules on Netflix if they were produced by Netflix's investment or exclusively broadcast by Netflix. These K-dramas are simultaneously streamed on Netflix as they are broadcast in Korea. These exclusively streamed or simulcast K-dramas receive the "Netflix Original" tag on both the Korean TV page and the main website. For instance, JTBC's drama, *MAN to MAN* and both *Live* and *Mr. Sunshine* by TVN (a Korean cable channel) are among the recent K-dramas released on Netflix via exclusive streaming. Usually, two episodes of these dramas are released each week, following the drama's Korean schedule. Most K-dramas on Netflix also provide different language options for subtitles, in addition to the English subtitles, depending on the territorial restrictions.

It is worth noting that the Netflix K-drama catalog reveals a commercial tendency of Netflix's selection standards for K-dramas, although Netflix's K-drama catalog relies heavily on licensing and copyright conditions. In this sense, the Korean drama catalog on Netflix is varied in terms of drama genres, international popularity, the lifecycle of the show, and the lengths of full episodes. All in all, Netflix has streamed K-dramas popular in many other countries, including those from the large Asian importers of K-dramas and also constantly offered Korean TV animations for kid's content as part of the Korean TV catalogs. Netflix provides streaming service for each K-drama within a licensed timeline, so on the old review boards some U.S. Netflix members complained about a show's frequent inaccessibility or asked for an extension or renewal for popular dramas. For example, some mega-hit K-dramas in many countries, such as *Moon Embraces the Sun*, *My Love from Another Star*, and *Goblin*, are often compared to other currently available dramas.

Netflix's previous selection of Korean TV shows tended not to be weighted toward certain genres or broadcasters, but since 2016 it has more often featured drama series from Korean cable channels that produce original series (e.g., TVN and OCN) and from a comprehensive channel, JTBC. With this new partnership, Netflix brings K-dramas into its catalog by adding new series based on crime, detective series, or thrillers—these genres are rare on Korean television and the popular genres consumed by U.S. television audiences—but recently both TVN and OCN have more produced such dramas in Korea. Moreover, some of JTBC's variety shows (e.g., *Hidden Singer*, *Men on a Mission*, and *Chef and My Fridge*) have made an appearance on Netflix. By early 2018, among the more than thirty K-dramas available on U.S. Netflix, only five dramas were produced by Korean network stations: *Descendants of the Sun* (KBS), *IRIS* (KBS), *Goodbye Mr. Black* (MBC),

White Nights (MBC), and *Boys Over Flowers* (KBS). This ties into Netflix's partnership agreement with CJ E&M as well as JTBC, as mentioned earlier. More importantly, it actually reflects Netflix's future direction in working with Korean television systems, especially outside of traditional broadcast networks in Korea.

DRAMAFEVER.COM: THE FIRST LEGAL STREAMING OF KOREAN TV SHOWS IN AMERICA

DramaFever.com is a legal online streaming site for licensed Asian TV content in North America, based in New York (Fujita 2014). It was the first legitimate online video streaming site serving Korean TV shows in the United States and officially launched in August 2009. The cofounders, Korean Americans Seung Bak and Suk Park, claimed in 2015 that the company had grown to be the largest online video distributor of international televised content with 21 million unique visitors, over 70 content partners, 14,000 episodes in their library, and 800 million minutes streamed per month (DramaFever 2015b, 2015c; Wong 2010). The company's success is closely related to the spread of the Korean Wave and the popularity of transnational K-dramas through localizing its fandom in the United States (Yu 2015).

In the beginning, DramaFever.com offered several Korean TV shows, nearly all drama series. DramaFever.com was the first online streaming provider that made licensing deals with all three Korean networks (KBS, MBC, and SBS) regarding their previous and current dramas. At first, DramaFever.com made an agreement with MBC to stream their dramas in the United States shortly after broadcast in Korea or even simultaneously with MBC's first domestic run. Then, SBS and KBS each agreed to stream their dramas through DramaFever.com in the United States (Ju 2017; Lee 2015). According to Lee (2015), only one month after the official launch of DramaFever.com in 2009, its regular users reached 200,000 and climbed to 4 million by April 2013. Suk Park said in an interview, "I think what we tapped into was the demand for foreign content regardless of your ethnic background. A demand for foreign content that was something different, something exciting, something interesting that wasn't available" (Fujita 2014). Regarding user demographics, DramaFever.com announced in 2017 that the majority of their users were women of color. Overall, 43 percent of these users were White, 27 percent Latino, 24 percent Asian, and 17 percent African American (Bai 2017). As the cofounders expected, DramaFever.com was successful in contacting dispersed online fan communities for Korean pop culture as well as the diasporic communities in the United States, meeting their desire for a new source of entertaining foreign TV content (Lee 2015).

American media companies are constantly seeking new kinds of TV shows and soon noticed the growing viewership of Korean TV shows via streaming platforms, along with DramaFever's rapidly growing membership. This led the company to start negotiations with U.S. media corporations to leverage its streaming business. First, in 2010 Hulu suggested a partnership with DramaFever.com to feature more than 200 K-dramas owned by DramaFever.com on the Hulu platform. Shortly afterward, several K-drama titles curated by DramaFever.com were made available on Netflix and iTunes as a result of a joint partnership (Fujita 2014; Ju 2017; Lee 2015). Moreover, DramaFever.com joined forces with one of Korea's leading production companies, Hwa & Dam Pictures, to produce its first original series, *Heirs*, which was domestically broadcast by SBS and achieved the highest TV ratings of 2013 in Korea (25.6%). DramaFever.com was the exclusive streaming platform for *Heirs*, simulcasting full episodes alongside the domestic TV schedule throughout the United States and Canada. Meanwhile the ownership of DramaFever.com has changed over the years. SoftBank bought the company in October 2014, increasing by tenfold the cofounders' initial investment in the company, and by the mid-2016 DramaFever.com had become a subsidiary of Warner Bros (Wikipedia 2018).

Different from Netflix, DramaFever provides two tiers of service: a free, ad-supported service without a membership or an ad-free premium subscription, offering high-definition access to any content in the catalog for a monthly fee. DramaFever.com extends its Asian TV offerings to include various programs from China, Taiwan, and Japan, but K-dramas along with K-star news still remain the key content (Lee 2015). In addition, it has been offering Spanish-language *telenovelas* from Argentina and Spain since late 2012, in order to better cater to Latino communities in the United States.

DramaFever.com holds the largest library of K-drama titles from Korean network stations as well as from some other cable companies such as TVN. It also streams some long-running popular K-dramas, such as daily family dramas and historic period dramas, that usually feature fifty episodes or more (compared with the 12–24 episodes of most K-dramas) to meet a broad range of members' needs. The main page of DramaFever.com includes the streaming drama and/or show catalogs, the related entertainment news (mostly regarding Korean drama entertainers, show updates, and K-pop news), and members' reviews and released episode recaps. The streaming content on the website is categorized by typical TV genre, such as romance, thriller, and fantasy, with the exclusive steaming content introduced as the primary content in the "only on DramaFever" category.

Interestingly, DramaFever.com subscribers can navigate all the shows offered and leave comments on a certain show or episode using the "recaps & reviews" board. Reviewers can interact with each other about the story recaps as well as share opinions about the stories and acting in a particular episode, forming an online community for the avid K-drama subscribers on the site. Subscribers' recaps and reviews are posted on the website and also shared via the DramaFever.com Facebook page.

To increase interactions with subscribers, DramaFever.com has also organized some offline events to encourage collective participation in promoting the streamed TV shows among their members. The company launched the "Annual DramaFever Awards" in 2013 to honor the films, dramas, actors, and actresses of the year, as selected by DramaFever subscribers' via an online vote (Wikipedia 2018). In addition, the company has participated in the annual Korean Wave convention, KCON, in Los Angeles or New York since 2016 and arranged the onsite event "DramaFever Red Carpet" to host popular Korean actors, actresses, and singers. Another irregular DramaFever.com Café Pop-Up event celebrates the release of new popular K-dramas. For example, when the K-drama *Goblin* was streamed on the site, 500 people attended an offline meeting event in New York in January 2017 to watch the last episode of the drama together (Bai 2017). In this sense, the DramaFever.com website functions not only as a streaming platform but also as a kind of Asian TV fan community online.

NOTES

1. Telenovela is a collective name for Spanish-language soap operas in Latin American countries. Telenovela series have dominated prime time broadcasting in these countries, especially Brazil, Mexico, and Columbia, and have been the primary source of television programming for the major broadcasters throughout Latin America. The popularity of telenovelas has extended to the areas where large Hispanic populations reside, such as the United States. For example, Telemundo serves the Spanish-speaking Hispanic populations across the United States, and telenovelas have also been exported to Europe, Africa, and the Middle East (Kim 2011, 370).

2. Joseph Straubharr (1991, 1996) brought to light the inter- or intra-regional media flows along with the cultural proximity thesis. He defined cultural proximity as the way transnational media content from a geographically adjacent region has greater influence on local audiences residing nearby. Straubharr argued that in terms of consuming imported TV programs, general audiences prefer more geo-culturally related programs to less geo-culturally related programs. He explained, "[The active audience are] tending to prefer and select local or national cultural content that is more proximate and relevant to them" (Straubharr 1991, 42). Also, Sinclair (1996a, 1996b) stressed evidence of cultural proximity in global media flow studies and found that the success of transnational media flows across the world goes beyond the factors of language differences. They include elements such as dress, nonverbal communication, humor, religion, music, and narrative style. According to Cunningham et al. (1998), "Audiences will first seek the pleasure of recognition of their own culture in

their program choices, and those programs will be produced to satisfy this demand, relative to the wealth of the market" (181).

3. Kim Eun-hee is one of the most popular TV screenwriters in Korea and she holds a great reputation for writing crime and thriller series, which are not common genres for weekly miniseries in Korea. A couple years ago she wrote the drama *Signal*, which aired on TVN between January and March in 2016. It was a mega-hit, breaking TVN's all-time drama ratings record (12.5%) (TVN drama homepage). *Signal* developed a story about a crime profiler in 2015 who happened to communicate with a detective living back in 1989 using a mysterious walkie-talkie, allowing the two to investigate a cold case together to find a real murderer, despite living twenty-six years apart. This drama was not only popularity but received fruitful acclaims from the public regarding the storyline's meaningful objective of searching for social justice.

Chapter 6

Korean Television Formats

Korean television programs, especially K-dramas, have moved transnationally, riding the Korean Wave. One important influence on this global mobility was a change in how Korean TV shows were traded internationally, beginning in the mid-2000s. Unlike in earlier years, both canned (or finished) TV programs and TV show formats started to be sold overseas at that time. More recently, the international trade of television programs includes the sale of a program form instead of a completed show (or series) itself: simply put, a TV program was licensed in other countries to be reproduced based on the original show format and storyline, an arrangement almost unheard of until the 1990s (Steemers, Iosifidis, and Wheeler 2005; Moran and Malbon 2006). Andrea Esser argued that the flow of television program formats, at both the national and international levels, became more significant in the 2000s, as TV format trade clearly increased at an international level between 2002 and 2004, then almost doubled between 2006 and 2008 at the international level (Esser 2010, 273–274).

Writ large, the television format trade is not a new phenomenon; however, TV format trade had not been at the forefront of the global media flows because the restricted media content flow was primarily driven from the United States or the United Kingdom toward other countries' media outlets. A few notable game shows and reality shows, such as *Who Wants to Be a Millionaire?*, *Survivor*, and *American Idol* (Chalaby 2016b), are the best examples of TV formats that were sold internationally. The recent rise of TV format trading took place in step with the transformation of a complex global media environment (Brennan 2010) and triggered the merging of national and international perspectives pertinent to transnational television flows, which notably include emerging non-Western or non-European TV formats. For example, the format of one Korean variety show was sold to and remade by Fox TV in the United States:

> A viral phenomenon with more than half a billion fans worldwide and the No. 1 top trending video of 2017 on YouTube, *The Masked Singer* features 12 celebrities singing competitively, while hidden under heavy crazy costumes over 10 episodes, the detectives try to figure out who the heck they are. (de Moreaes 2018)

This is not the first case of a U.S. remake within Korean television's variety and entertainment genres, but it does demonstrate the unexpected success of a Korean TV format on U.S. television. Typically, TV format trades have taken advantage of a few genres, such as talent shows, studio games, and quiz shows, that earn more audience attention to as well as advertising profits compared to other genres. These entertainment shows' formats also tend to be easy to remake in different countries, adopting various local themes and topics alongside the original format. Likewise, themes of beauty, fame, and wealth comprise the main trend of this entertainment show format internationally, which can be readily represented through relatively low-budget productions in many national broadcast systems (Brennan 2012). Certainly, the TV format market on an international scale reveals the great flexibility of entertainment show formats, so they can be adopted in broad and successful deals between national broadcasters.

In recent years, television formats around the world have grown rapidly in terms of their volume and scope of circulation compared to previous years (FRAPA and Mckenzie 2017), and more importantly more diverse TV genres beyond the popular entertainment shows are likely to be traded as new TV formats. Chalaby (2016b) demonstrated that both non-scripted (e.g., variety and reality shows) and scripted genres (e.g., soap operas and drama series) are of interest for local adaptation in the international TV format trade. In this growing market, Korean television programs have also exhibited a noted increase for both Korean TV dramas and variety shows. More TV program buyers from different countries, including Western countries, seek K-dramas they can remake locally into a new series or format. Therefore, this chapter outlines the emerging Korean television formats in transnational television markets and sheds light on the impact of K-drama (and Korean TV shows more broadly) formats in the United States and the United Kingdom. In this light, the current nature of transnational Korean television effectively shows the change and innovation of Korean television programing, genres, and transnational strategies.

TELEVISION FORMAT: HOW DOES IT WORK INTERNATIONALLY?

While the term *television format* is commonly used in TV production and distribution, it's not easy to define a format precisely. The term originated in the print industry where it measured a specific page size and then the concept of a format extended first to radio and later to television, where it was tied to the principal of serial program production (Moran and Keane 2004). More specifically, Moran (2004, 5) narrowly defined a television format as "a set of invariable elements in a program out of which the variable elements of an individual episode are produced. Equally, a format can be seen as a means of organizing individual episodes." Moran's definition focuses on TV format in terms of programming elements for creating each episode, but only when it is adopted by other countries' broadcasters. However, more recent scholarship has suggested a new approach, defining TV format in consideration of the overall protocols for a television content trade driven by a deregulated commercial media system.

This definition brings up an extended discussion about how TV format relates to the methods of circulating television programs internationally. Specifically, TV formats may go beyond programming elements to include either unscripted or fully scripted exchanges to be remade by local media, along with production-related knowledge and know-how, services, and other production aspects from the original program (Brennan 2012; Chalaby 2016b; Esser 2010; Keane 2008). In turn, TV format trades in today's television industry are likely to require more than the program itself. TV format sales on the international market feature a range of licensing deals, depending on the production condition of the importing nation's broadcast system, without any fundamental tampering with the structure of the original program. As the result of this extended concept of TV formats, broadcasters around the world are granted a wide scope of pre- and postproduction knowledge, along with elaborate production instructions from the original format, when they trade for a TV format. This production-related knowledge necessarily includes systemic knowledge outside of TV program elements, so the television industry refers to this as a production bible.

In this context, it has been agreed that a TV format in today's global television industry indicates the sum of the essential elements to generate the central characteristics of a program in production—a recipe with all the necessary ingredients to produce a TV program (Brennan 2012). Broadcast executives involved in international sales have remarked that TV formats more recently have embraced the extended components of programming, including the concretization of an idea sold in the form of a production bible from the format exporter, as well as a compilation of production knowledge in order to ease the remake for the format importer (Brennan 2012; Chalaby 2016b). TV format trades often include a certain type of production bible covering technical requirements, lessons learned, a shooting schedule, crew list, budget sample, and any other valuable strategic plans for the production team (Esser 2010, 274), above and beyond the original scripts, special effects, and audiovisual elements for the narrative.

Taken all together, the Format Recognition and Protection Association (FRAPA) notes that TV formats are licensed assets by the production company creating a particular TV program. No doubt, FRAPA considers TV formats as licensable commodities in the broadcasting industry and the currently soaring format trade makes up a significant part of the international television market (FRAPA and Mckenzie 2017). FRAPA was founded in 2000 to support and manage international TV or film trades, especially in protecting the format rights of broadcast corporations and production houses across the world (FRAPA 2011). It is an international organization run by members associated with TV and film production companies around the world, and its members' copyright infringement cases regarding TV format trades have been closely monitored.

TV formats are composed of several categories of creative works under copyright law, including separate copyrights for literary, artistic, musical, and dramatic works. In the context of a television drama or variety show, literary copyright will protect the script; artistic copyright will protect the storyboard, set-design, layout, and any on-screen graphical elements; and musical copyright will protect the opening theme or other music created for the show. However, FRAPA found that apart from the music and graphical elements, TV formats on scripted shows are better protected by literary copyrights, whereas non-scripted reality or variety shows seem harder to protect from a legal perspective (FRAPA 2011). Not surprisingly, network stations and television production companies in the Western media marketplace have been associated with FRAPA since its foundation because of their prolific TV format trade between European countries or from the United States (or the United Kingdom) to other territories. Latin American and Asian countries joined FRAPA relatively late, mostly entering in the past few years, showing that TV format trade has become broader and more diverse as it connects the broadcast industry in global contexts. The three Korean network stations (e.g., KBS, MBC, and SBS) and a number of large TV/film production firms in Korea have been members of FRAPA since 2012, triggered by a rise of Korean TV format trade in the global television industry.

The success of TV formats relies heavily on how much they can appeal internationally and be capable of recreation as local versions of programs. In essence, television is a visual and emotional medium: the emotive nature of television does not greatly differ for global audiences anywhere, so a remake of a TV format can create and develop similar (or different) emotional arousals among transnational audiences in numerous ways. Therefore, broadcasters and television content creators try to take advantage of a few successful TV genres that seem to emotionally engage a broader range of audience groups, even as they edit the original format with different social, political, and lifestyle themes. In fact, this rationale for the growth of the TV format trade explains why drama series, soap operas, reality, and variety shows have been circulating and reproducing better than other TV programs in cross-border contexts. Using these genres may increase the chance to appeal to audiences overseas through a format rather than a completed (or canned) program. Often, the popular TV formats around the world try to convey a simple but emotionally moving message associated with what is valued by individual audiences thinking of the good life (Brennan 2012).

The *Betty* format demonstrates the phenomenal international success of a scripted TV format beyond the Western-dominated TV formats (e.g., game, talent, or reality shows). Hilmes (2013) investigated the transnational trajectory of the *Betty* format and stressed that a series of *Betty* formats marked a unique moment in the globalization of television through its remarkable success from nation to nation. *Betty* formats set a record for local remakes of the original telenovela version, appearing in more than thirty-three languages and across virtually every geographical region. The origin of the *Betty* format is a Columbian telenovela, *Yo Soy Betty, La Fea*, produced by RCN. After its first run in Columbia, it was licensed for eighteen local adaptations in Latin American countries (Esser 2010). Later in 2006, the ABC network in the United States started broadcasting its remake *Ugly Betty*, which aired for four more seasons on ABC. Interestingly, *Ugly Betty* also aired in more than ninety countries and at least twenty versions had been made as of 2013 (Chalaby 2016b, 14). Nonetheless, the *Betty* format, including *Ugly Betty*, stands for not only a scripted format's success (a serial drama) but also the potential of telenovelas (Latin American style of TV dramas) in global television marketplaces.

While TV formats have increased and shown the commercial value of distribution in global television flows, many broadcasters and content distributors believe that scripted TV shows, such as dramas, soap operas, or sitcoms, are more challenging to adapt than the relatively less complex unscripted shows. However, the demand for more scripted format shows has been growing. Chalaby (2016b) noted that scripted television shows are the most difficult to adapt in foreign countries due to the complexity of the knowledge transfer during production. Scripted genres demand a recreation of the original format in terms of culturally sensitive storytelling, to attract local audiences who will consume the remade show. By the same token, in a finished (or canned) program trade, both comedy and drama series have proven to be relatively difficult in overcoming cultural accents and nuances, so these scripted genres can't be easily received by international audiences.

In this vein, scripted TV formats may not expect a high reception from local audiences if they are reproduced as mechanistically as unscripted TV formats—such as a game show or talent competition—can be developed. A straight adaptation of the original drama or sitcom script from other countries will not suffice to make the remade show palatable to local viewers (Chalaby 2016b). The scripted TV formats rather require a fuller cultural translation and interpretation of the original script to suit the local culture and audience tastes apart from the format itself, and if a remake of scripted TV formats isn't recreated well, the risk of failure is substantially higher than with unscripted TV formats. Especially in terms of cultural sensitivity, scripted TV formats within the scope of a broadcast organization may not be effective in adapting a local remake quickly enough to meet the broadcaster's intended time line. To be sure, recreating drama or sitcom formats takes some time, as to succeed they must make sense in local contexts and have suitable narratives for recreation (Chalaby 2016b). It is not rare to see a foreign drama format canceled during the actual process of a remake because the resulting production delays inevitably incur increases in production costs. For example, the mega-hit Korean drama *My Love From Another Star* was sold to the United States by ABC and greenlit for a remake in 2014, but the remade pilot didn't even make the cut for ABC's regular TV season in the following year's lineup (Lee and Szalai 2016).

Whatever the projected hurdles, both scripted and unscripted TV formats offer two benefits for the broadcast industry. First, TV formats can provide a cost-effective production based on a ready-made script, enabling production companies to bring down the cost involved with the development of an original program. Second, broadcasters can effectively manage the possible risks of a remade show not being commercially successful, thanks to the relatively low production budgets compared to a creation of an original show (Chalaby 2016b).

KOREAN TELEVISION FORMATS IN THE UNITED STATES: DRAMAS AND VARIETY SHOWS

In the Korean television industry, TV dramas have long been the most precious business entity because of the genre's high advertising revenue based on competitive viewing ratings. Korean network stations (KBS, MBC, and SBS) had significant power over independent production firms and cable stations when it came to producing TV dramas, mainly for two reasons: the TV networks had the financial stability to budget for original drama production and the capability to air the dramas on their terrestrial channels. In the mid-2000s, however, Korean network stations began to face heavier competition in the domestic TV market from high-profile cable stations (e.g. OCN and

TVN) and new comprehensive TV channels, such as JTBC and TV Chosun, all of which can afford to produce their own original drama series and variety shows, many of which are among the most popular and loved TV shows among domestic audiences (Ju 2017). Given this more intense competition, TV formats, especially those of dramas and variety shows, have spurred interest in a new segment of content distribution to sell outside the country. By targeting the international market, sales of a finished TV drama continue to be promoted, and in the meantime the format sale of both K-dramas and variety shows reaches a new and valuable pipeline for international markets.

Table 6.1 summarizes the format sale of K-dramas since 2006. As shown, China has been the largest buyer of K-drama formats for more than a decade, followed by other Asian countries, such as Vietnam, Thailand, and the

Table 6.1 Korean TV Format Trade: TV Drama Series

Genre	Title	Year of Sales	Countries
Drama Series	Delightful Girl Choon-Hyang	2006; 2009	China; Vietnam
	Hotelier	2007	Japan
	My Girl	2007	Indonesia
	All about Eve	2008	Vietnam
	Coffee Prince	2008; 2010	Philippines; Taiwan
	Full House	2008	Vietnam, Philippines
	My Name Is Kim Sam Soon	2008	Philippines
	Queen of Games	2008	China
	Stairway to Haven	2008	Philippines
	Infamous Seven Princesses	2009	China; Vietnam
	Smile You	2009	China
	Autumn Fairy Tale	2010	Philippines
	Successful Story of a Bright Girl	2010	Taiwan
	Temptation of a Wife	2010; 2012; 2013	China; Philippines; Turkey
	Sorry and Love You	2012	Japan
	My Love from Another Star	2014	China; United States
	Nine	2013	United States
	God's Gift: 14 days	2013	United States
	Good Doctor	2014	United States
	Misaeng: Incomplete Life	2015	Japan
	Kill Me Heel Me	2016	China
	Oh My Ghost	2016	Thailand
	Who Are You	2016	United Kingdom
	Signal	2016	Japan
	Descendants of the Sun	2016	Vietnam
	When a Man Falls in Love	2016	Mexico
	Glamorous Temptation	2016	Mexico

Source: Data was collected from multiple sources and was reorganized by the author: see ABC Entertainment 2017; Andreeva 2016; de Moraes 2018; Goldberg 2014, 2016; Jeon, A. 2017; Jeon 2017; Jin 2016, 56; Joo 2016; Korea Creative Content Agency 2011, 2014b, 2015; Lee and Szalai 2016; Levin 2017; Wagmeister 2016.

Philippines. This data reveals a continuous regional interest in purchasing K-drama and/or variety show formats for local remakes. Until 2012, K-drama formats were spread throughout Asian television via the Korean Wave, which was particularly driven by some phenomenal dramas in romance genres. Interestingly, among the Asian countries, Japan has recently been most active in remaking K-drama formats in their own versions: *Sorry and Love You* (2012), *Miseang* (2015), and *Signal* (2016) were all reproduced in Japan after the first remake of the K-drama format, *Hotelier*, back in 2007. Japan was one of the largest buyers of K-dramas previously, but their interest in purchasing finished K-dramas has waned, in contrast to the resurrection of interest in the format of K-dramas. More significantly, this trend by Japanese broadcasters to remake K-dramas focuses more on their particular interest in the original K-drama stories about serious social and political problems that resonate in Japanese society.

Since 2013, the format sales of Korean TV shows have shown a pattern of globalization outside the Asian market. Thus, broadcasters are likely to trade K-drama formats with the United States and the United Kingdom. When considering the relationships of media content trade between Korea and the United States, Korean TV program exports to the United States are still meager, while Korean networks and cable stations have long preferred to import American TV series:

> In terms of the media and entertainment (M&E) industry, South Korea has maintained a good trading relationship with the United States—the largest M&E market in the world. The US M&E export to South Korea increased from $393.11 million in 2014 to $465.67 million in 2016. Many Korean remakes of US TV series—such as *Saturday Night Live*, *The Good Wife*, and *Criminal Minds*—have drawn huge viewerships. (Kim 2017)

The U.S. series *Suits* (by USA Network) is the most recent example of a Korean remake. In 2017, the Korean commercial network SBS recreated the drama and aired it with the same title as the original U.S. series. However, the Korean remake of *Suits* was only broadcast for a single sixteen-episode season, unlike the original series. Korean audiences positively responded to the remake and many online discussions compared it with the original U.S. series. In Korea, remakes of American TV series are unusual, especially by the networks. However, Korean cable channels have sometimes decided to purchase American TV formats of dramas or reality shows to recreate them with relatively low production budgets. In this case, the U.S. series holds certain domestic fans so their active viewership can call attention to a Korean remake version.

Gradually, K-drama formats have developed a new relationship between the Korean and U.S. television industries, and international sales of K-drama formats have lately reached the United States, Latin America, and Europe. This indicates that Western TV buyers better recognize the continuous popularity of Korean television programs over the past decade, starting in Asia, and have started to consider not only finished K-dramas but also the potential of popular Korean TV formats. The following media interview explains the rise of Korean TV formats in the Western television market:

> According to Angela Killoren, COO at CJ E&M America, "The real popularity of K-drama started from just the original dramas being made accessible online. Then people started hearing about these incredible numbers—millions of people a month out of the U.S. and all these countries outside Korea watching, and people were very intrigued." And that has led to interest in remakes. (Lee and Szalai 2016)

Internal market change in U.S. television is another reason why K-drama formats can enter that market. As discussed previously, unscripted game and reality shows are major global TV formats while the drama genres do not travel well internationally. Nonetheless, U.S. television networks need to find a new source of TV programs as they are running out of fresh subjects to feed their channels. It is worth noting that many U.S. channels have long been occupied by similar entertainment genres, such as reality shows; this is the premier factor driving the sizable expansion of drama genres on U.S. television. Likewise, new players in the U.S. television market have developed an interest in scripted genres that appeal better than the traditional purveyors of drama, the U.S. networks. HBO's success becomes the model that many other new channels follow, and cable channels such as AMC, Bravo, FX, Pivot, Showtime, and TLC have started making drama series to possess their own original exclusive content (White 2013).

Furthermore, the overall demand for drama genres and new scripts has sharply increased in America. Again, the U.S. networks' competitors, the so-called online streaming TV platforms such Netflix and Lovefilm.com, have been more successful in developing original drama series (Chalaby 2016b). Faced with this renewed internal competition, the U.S. networks themselves have turned their efforts toward making more investments in scripted shows, including both drama series and foreign scripted shows. Given this transformation, the U.S. content aggregators must inevitably diversify their programming sources, and foreign TV remakes seem to be more adaptable in terms of content and production, compared to investing in the creation of an original scripted show (Chalaby 2016b).

The first K-drama format sold to the United States was *God's Gift-14 Days* (2014), which was a fourteen-episode crime thriller about a mother searching for the suspected murderer of her kidnapped daughter. The thriller is a favored genre on American television, so ABC network purchased the format of the K-drama, recreating it as a ten-episode series entitled *Somewhere Between* in the summer of 2017 (Andreeva 2016; Goldberg 2016; Wagmeister 2016). As the result of unsuccessful viewing ratings for the full ten-episode series, ABC cancelled the show's regular season broadcast. Another K-drama format adoption by ABC was the remake of the K-drama *My Love From Another Star* in 2014. This time ABC wanted to consult with the Korean writer of the original script to remake a well-adapted U.S. series. As noted, TV format trade is considered as more of a knowledge transfer (Chalaby 2016b), including detailed production know-how. In the case *My Love From Another Star*, the writer of the original script, Park Ji-eun, was brought on board as an executive producer in order to facilitate the comprehensive knowledge transfer of the original K-drama (Lee and Szalai 2016). The U.S. remake was coproduced by HB Entertainment and EnterMedia Contents in association with Sony Pictures Television (Goldberg 2014). However, in the end, the remake of *My Love From Another Star* did not make it through the preseason screening of ABC's new dramas. Unfortunately, ABC's two attempts to remake K-drama formats did not lead to successful broadcasts.

This failure demonstrates the difficulty of adapting a drama series from foreign scripts where the local culture of foreign audience is more distant from the sense of K-drama narratives. Indeed, foreign TV dramas require careful handling when they are remade by different local television networks, and the entire production needs a lot of careful story development and presentation techniques to localize the cultural accents embedded in the original format. Without an advanced adaptation by local broadcasters, a remake of a foreign TV drama won't easily be well received by local audiences, so transnational viewership data is less certain to guarantee the local success of a remake of a foreign TV drama (Chalaby 2016b).

Another Korean drama format, however, produced a contrasting result and has been successful on U.S. television. In 2014, ABC purchased a K-drama format entitled *The Good Doctor*. The U.S. remake (which kept the title) actually took almost three years to air on ABC, with the first of the thirteen episodes launching in September 2017. The drama was ranked the U.S. networks' number one new drama in the 2017 fall season and ABC immediately ordered five more episodes to complete the first full season. In early 2018, ABC decided to continue with a second season of *The Good Doctor* on the 2018 fall schedule (ABC Entertainment 2017; Kim 2017). This medical drama is about the life journeys of a young surgeon with autism and savant syndrome who joins a surgical unit in a prestigious hospital in a large city. ABC's remake retains the primary narratives and plot arcs of the original K-drama, maintaining high character synchronicity with the Korean version. The original K-drama delivered a heartwarming story highlighting the main character's growth in becoming a real surgeon while fighting prejudices toward mental disabilities in his highly professional world. When Korean domestic viewers watched the original drama, they got deeply involved in how the lead male character's autism made him face enormous problems in communicating and relating well with doctors, patients, and other professionals. In the end, the K-drama touched viewers' emotions by showing his innocent personality and his desire to take care of people as a warmhearted surgeon.

Overall, *The Good Doctor* in the U.S. remake tells a similar story, but the U.S. version focuses more on the personal change of individual characters as they get through different medical cases. When the U.S. remake adopted the original script, the relationships that the protagonist developed with other doctors, staff, and patients were well translated to appeal better to U.S. viewers. Specifically, the first episode of the U.S. remake greatly resembles the same episode of the Korean version in terms of sequences and events. One memorable scene in the first episode is of the protagonist saving a child's life with his fast but accurate diagnosis and skillful emergency treatment (see figure 6.1). This scene represents an important event where audiences can grasp the protagonist's genius and talents regardless of his autism disability. This event attracts viewers' attention to the protagonist's personality and his savant syndrome, along with his autism, and encourages the audience to relate and sympathize more with the protagonist as they heartily cheer him on.

As seen in figure 6.1, the scene looks very similar in terms of the characters' postures, their actions, and even the spectators' positions. The camera angles slightly differ in the U.S. remake, and in the American version the accident happens at an airport instead of the train station in the original. This alteration shows attention to lifestyle differences between Korea and America. Overall, the success of *The Good Doctor* indicates that remaking a medical drama—one of the most popular TV genres in America—was a good decision. The original scripts and main theme are adopted meticulously to cater to the American viewers' needs, while the characterization of a surgeon with autism was thoroughly developed based on the original K-drama. In particular, the U.S. remake deals with many different medical cases in the general surgical unit, in order to extend the series beyond one season, while the original K-drama set all the episodes in the series in the pediatric surgical unit.

As shown in table 6.2, K-dramas are not the only content in the growing international trade of Korean TV formats; Korean variety shows (an entertainment genre including reality shows, talent shows, and travel shows) also account for a significant portion of the format trade. U.S. remakes of these variety shows have appeared more frequently than remakes of K-dramas, especially since 2016. As with the K-drama format, though,

Figure 6.1 Scene: Saving a Kid's Life in *The Good Doctor*—Original Korean Drama versus the U.S. Remake. *Source*: Screenshot by the Author (Original Korean Drama vs. U.S. Remake).

China has been the most active buyer of Korean variety show formats. This has happened since 2011, as it is easier and cost-efficient for Chinese networks to remake Korean variety shows and license them in local versions, so they can produce more entertainment shows in a short period of time. Accordingly, many Chinese remakes of Korean variety shows have been well received by their local viewers because of the huge popularity of all kinds of K-dramas there.

Table 6.2 Korean TV Format Trade: Variety Shows

Title	Year of Sales	Countries
Match Made in Heaven	2006	China
Golden Bell	2006; 2008	Vietnam; China
I Am a Singer	2011	China
We Got Married	2011; 2013; 2014	China; Turkey
Super Star K	2011; 2013	China
Dad, Where Are We Going?	2013	China
One Night Two Days (Season 1)	2013	China
Audition of Miracle	2013	China
The Romantic	2013	China
Superman Came Back	2014	China
Immortal Song	2014	China
Grandpa Over Flowers	2014	China; Italy; United States; Turkey
K-pop Star (Season 1)	2014	China
Hidden Singer	2014	China
Real Man	2014	China
Celebrities in my House	2014	China
My In-law's home	2014	China
Infinite Challenge	2015	China
The Masked Singer	2015–2016	China; Thailand; India; United States
Sisters Over Flowers	2015	China
I Can See Your Voice	2015	China
Let's Go Time Expedition	2015	China
Off to School	2015	China
Take Care of My Dad	2016	China United States

Source: Data was collected from multiple sources and reorganized by the author: see Andreeva 2016; de Moraes 2018; Jeon 2017; Jin 2016, 56; Joo 2016; Korea Creative Content Agency 2011, 2014b, 2015.

The first Chinese remake of a Korean variety show format was the popular singing competition *I Am a Singer*. The Chinese version changed nothing from the original, including the title, studio design, competition rules, and behind-the-scenes features on competitors. Chinese television viewers were already familiar with the so-called super formats, such as *Britain's Got Talent* and *American Idol*, before many Korean formats of variety shows arrived, and a considerable number of viewers had already seen Western-style competition and/or talent shows. However, *I Am a Singer* used a new format: currently popular professional singers participate in a singing competition every week, and the individual with the lowest votes on the day of competition is eliminated from the competition. With this fresh show format the Chinese remake was highly successful, getting famous and being acclaimed by local viewers when the remake aired. This success triggered continuous increases in Chinese broadcasters' remaking Korean variety show formats. It can be said that the TV formats of both K-drama and Korean variety shows have formed an essential part of Chinese television programs.

Unlike K-drama formats, unscripted genres such as Korean variety shows are regularly offered with full access to the consulting packages of the original show, so foreign broadcasters know how to duplicate the show successfully as a local version. To meet the increased demand, buyers of foreign TV formats have requested more detailed processes regarding the show itself, so in this sense the production bible is necessary to make a deal. Currently Korean variety show formats tend to provide with both a show's production bible and so-called flying producers, who assist with on-site consults for foreign TV production teams when a format is remade locally (Chalaby 2016b; Esser 2010). The importance of the production bible lies in the concrete information about an original show's production knowledge, technical skill sets, and other strategic tips for a successful production process. As Chalaby (2016b, 15) notes, this entire process of Korean variety show formats can be a part of knowledge transfer in the general TV format trade. Knowledge transfer has especially improved recently in Korean variety show formats, where producers develop on-site studio support for a remake production that includes on-site assistance to the local production team, so the remade show will get on the air efficiently to garner more attention from the local audience. Because the viewership of a local remake is always uncertain, the improved knowledge transfer facilitates effective and rapid remake production, so the risks of a remake tend to be managed better.

In the United States, two Korean variety show formats have been adopted well for U.S. television: *Better Late Than Never* (NBC in 2017) and *The Masked Singer* (Fox in 2018). *Better Late Than Never* is a remake of the most famous Korean reality show, *Grandpa Over Flowers*, which has proven popular in many other countries. Likewise, NBC's remake recorded the top viewing ratings in the time slot during its first season, so NBC approved a second season (Jeon 2017). Meanwhile, *Grandpa Over Flowers* has continued for four seasons (with a ten-episode show each season) in Korea for over five years, and TVN, the show's production company, asserted that it was a phenomenal success in Korean reality show history. Before the show's format was adapted in the United States, it had already appeared in some local versions in other countries, including China, Italy, and Turkey (Jeon 2017).

The original show is based on a real travel story of four elderly Korean actors (over seventy years old, on average) and a younger male actor who serves as the caregiver for all four elders to keep their foreign travels running smoothly. The elders' free and natural travel story and their long-term friendships really touched Korean audiences, while their unexpected experiences while sightseeing in different foreign countries also provided natural emotions and cool feelings for a large audience. In addition, the younger actor, who is in charge of driving, cooking, and caring for the elders on their travels, produced many funny and memorable moments that harmonized well with the free travel concept of the show. For Western TV format buyers, this show can appeal to much of their domestic audience in the same way that Korean viewers were moved.

Fox TV is broadcasting another U.S. remake of a Korean show, *The Masked Singer*, keeping the original title. It uses a familiar singing competition format, but all the competitors wear special costumes and masks to hide their identities until they are eliminated from competition. Nearly all the competitors are popular celebrities. Fox's remade show follows the main elements of the original Korean show. However, while the Korean show plays up the intrigue of guessing which celebrity is under each mask while they're singing, the Fox version seems to be focused on pleasing American viewers with the extravagant masks and costumes (de Moraes 2018). MBC produced the original show in 2015 and has continued to broadcast it with relatively high ratings. Interestingly, both U.S. remakes (*Better Late Than Never* and *The Masked Singer*) were up and running on the air quickly after the format was purchased; this tells us that unscripted Korean TV formats have more potential to be adapted well in the United States or in broader global television markets.

Above all, the Korean TV format trade has been accelerating and aiming more and more at broader television markets overseas, even considering the United States. The Korean broadcast industry encourages this trend in two ways. First, the Korean broadcast and entertainment industry connect to foreign media companies through joint ventures, coproduction, and media trade partnerships. For example, Korean entertainment giant CJ E&M (TVN's parent company) made partnerships with Chinese, Singaporean, and Vietnamese broadcasters to coproduce local versions of successful Korean variety shows. Foreign partnerships generate joint ventures for Korean television production systems, so Korean production companies have more foreign investment, particularly in the creation of new dramas and shows. Often these foreign partnerships result not only in a sale of a finished show but also TV format sales of new shows targeting the partnered media markets. This helps to expand the scope of Korean TV shows and formats abroad, along with joint ventures or advertising sponsorships (Lee 2014).

Second, Korean networks and high-profile cable channels broaden their original show promotions on a more global scale and Western television markets are no longer an exception to this tendency. For instance, CJ E&M America is actively involved in a trade with U.S. television buyers for both finished programs and formats of Korean TV shows. A couple of Korean TV formats have succeeded in getting attention from American viewers, and CJ E&M and other Korean production companies recognize such valuable TV formats in their program line-up. The National Association of Television Program Executives (NATPE) organizes an annual convention, held in major cities of the United States, which serves as an international crossroads meeting for the buyers and sellers of television programming (Bielby and Harrington 2008). According to the Korea Creative Content Association, since 2016 the three Korean networks, CJ E&M, and JTBC have all participated in the NATPE Market & Conference to feature their original drama series and formats at promotional screening events (Joo 2016).

Along similar lines, these major Korean television stations have showcased their original dramas and variety shows alongside the format sales, for foreign program buyers at the annual MIP-TV convention in Cannes, France. MIPCOM and MIP-TV are the Reed MIDEM Organization of France's annual fall and spring transnational TV content events in Cannes (Bielby and Harrington 2008, 2); MIPFORMATS is a promotional exhibition at MIP-TV focusing on international TV format trade. MIPFORMATS has offered a great opportunity to promote Korean TV formats overall since 2014 (Jeon 2017). In short, the growing visibility of Korean TV formats in international television circuits, including the major TV fairs, illustrates an increasing awareness of Korean television content and its commercial value for different broadcast locales.

Conclusion

Transnational television flows and their evolving roles in different local and/or national television are deeply interconnected with multilayered global media mechanisms and the dynamics of geo-cultural media division. Korean TV dramas and non-drama programs, in recent years, have played an important role in diversifying transnational TV flows around the world. Despite much attention from academia, cultural institutions, and the entertainment industry, however, previous studies on these topics are insufficient to map out the past and current paths of transnational Korean television. Even as academic discussions about the Korean Wave have heated up, transnational studies of Korean television from transnational viewpoints often lack in-depth analysis and often overlook the extended flow of Korean television beyond Asia.

A few empirical audience studies, based on local viewers' reception behaviors and consumption tendencies, have called attention to the critical role of Korean TV dramas in the Korean Wave phenomena. To build on this work, in this book I provide previously absent analyses of K-dramas' transnational influences, peculiar production features, distribution, and consumption, producing several significant theoretical implications. This project enriches our knowledge of Korean dramas' transnational and/or transcultural forms, narratives, and commercial and noncommercial paths to reach overseas audiences. As discussed through all six chapters of this book, Korean TV dramas have pioneered the international mobility of Korean media and pop culture in a broad scope. They constantly expand the Korean media industry, flowing out with the globalization of the Korean broadcasting system, internal industry and market changes, new governing policies and institutions, and the technological transformation of audiences.

This study's significant findings and implications should be recognized and elaborated on for future transnational Korean media studies. First, the analysis of transnational flows of Korean TV dramas is valuable in tracing the evolutionary nature of the Korean Wave over the past few decades. Korean dramas consumed overseas likewise demonstrate the internal and external transformation of Korean media systems and the converging platform technologies. Meanwhile, the scales of transnational Korean television suggest that the entertainment economy depends on changing tastes of audiences and the popularity cycle of Korean television abroad. The phases of evolution in transnational Korean television flows accompany both continuities and discontinuities of content streams, along with intensive connections among national, regional, and global media industries in terms of production, distribution, and consumption.

Moreover, Korean dramas' international popularity has grown with the entire East Asian television market, as examined in chapter 1, which transformed rapidly in response to the neoliberal ideologies driving the worldwide cultural globalization at the end of the 1990s. In accordance with East Asia's regional milieu, Korean television programs inflows surged into the Asian region and triggered the increase of reciprocal media exchanges as examined in chapter 3, while domestically restructuring the capability of Korean television content and enhancing the entire mechanism of production and distribution. Particularly before 2010, some analysts simply concluded that the Korean television industry was able to shore up the export of Korean TV dramas to neighboring countries mainly by relying on their governmental intervention and support. As a result, the activated governmental support for Korea's domestic media industry was called a soft power policy, but this political meaning has been overemphasized to explain the substance of transnationalism in Korean television.

In this respect, the coevolved media globalization of neighboring Asian countries has been overlooked, especially the fact that these nations made their own strategic decisions to buy Korean TV dramas due to the dramas' cost-efficient benefits in their own marketplaces. In those Asian countries, the domestic cost of imported Korean dramas was relatively cheaper than the cost of other major imports from Japan or the United States. Additionally, Asian regional viewers responded enormously well to the brief circulation of Korean dramas, compared to competing shows. Neighboring Asian countries' increased imports of Korean TV dramas took advantage of reduced TV program costs to feed many channels while increasing advertising revenue, thanks to their viewers' great responses. In other words, previous policy-driven analyses on transnational Korean television flows oversimplified the success of Korean dramas' Asian-centered flows by relying only on a single factor (government institutional power) and by restricting their attention to national media systems. Instead, the emerging transnational flows of Korean drama require a much more complex and sophisticated theoretical model, as this flow is constantly changing the scope of territoriality and converging technologies.

Second, a number of case studies pertinent to transnational Korean TV dramas underline the significant impact of Korean dramas' thematic and semiotic narratives on transnational audiences' reception and consumption patterns. More importantly, the heart of K-dramas' transnational popularity stems from their transnational viewers and avid fans being able to access multiple digital platforms. While some previous audience studies on K-dramas addressed the active participatory culture among dispersed transnational consumers of Korean drama through online media, they rarely focused on the specific modes of consumption and reception typical to Korean dramas. Transnational viewers and fans of Korean dramas testify to their affective involvement in the dramas' distinct narratives and ways of storytelling from their own ethno-cultural points of view.

In this light, future research on transnational Korean drama consumption should be shaped by investigating how online consumption of Korean dramas among overseas viewers (including fans) differently influences their affective engagement in the televised components of Korean drama texts and images, an important departure from the traditional broadcast audience studies. The Web and streaming platforms give instant access to much international TV content and these online viewing experiences can immediately connect audiences to other viewers or fans across borders. Online viewers' behaviors when consuming Korean dramas tend to illustrate some differences to conventional habits, such as binge watching or repetitive watching, but thus far few reception or fan studies about transnational Korean dramas have elaborated on the distinct affective engagement in the drama narratives or how the online communicative practices crossing borders.

As fandom is an essential process for incorporating and associating with the primary sources of foreign cultures and mediated symbolic identities, in the case of Korean dramas transnational online TV fandom greatly contributes to constructing regional and global circles of allegiance among its viewers, often by means of various forms of viral messages. YouTube, Netflix, DramaFever, and other local or region-based streaming platforms form a connected digital community for transnational Korean drama consumers. More importantly, I argue that both reception and fan studies of transnational Korean dramas demand the advancement of applicable analytic methodologies to better explain the dominant pattern of online and streaming viewership.

On a more practical level, I think that online viewers' and fans' reviews and discussion dialogues, from both streaming and fan-based websites, should be accurately employed in audience reception studies. This type of data has not been seriously dealt with in current TV audience studies because it's been considered too subjective to incorporate as the primary data set in media reception studies. In reality, though, Korean dramas have been consumed online by a majority of transnational audiences and their online responses engage the feelings, emotions, reactions, and learned knowledge as a result of watching a Korean drama. This approach highlights the value of understanding online television viewership in global contexts and can alleviate the lack of both immediacy and unfiltered sensibility about viewers' communications, both potential problems with the ethnographic data analyzed in previous television audience studies. Media scholarship should produce sharper analysis on the actual ways transnational audiences engage with certain international TV content, incorporating discussion boards online as well as streaming platforms within audience research, rather than ignoring or devaluing this type of data.

According to the majority of reception studies, Korean TV dramas are popular in Asian countries because these Asian viewers or fans enjoyed the mixed experiences of decoding and interpreting Korean dramas and because they believed in a cultural dyad of East vs. West. These individuals enjoyed knowing and experiencing cross-cultural lives to experience burgeoning global pop culture and lifestyles and consuming images and stories delivered by Korean dramas are part of this new entertainment desire. In this vein, the cultural hybridity theory—an antithetical approach to the complexity of global media flows—is often used to explain Korean dramas' transnational fandom.

Of course, cultural hybridity theory can be useful to underline Korean dramas' transnational reception or participatory culture by couching entertainment behaviors in terms of cultural and ethnic consumption. However, this approach misses the fact that Western audiences who mainly receive Korean dramas through online platforms do not seriously take into account the narratives and symbolic textual meanings based on a comparative cultural view contrasting Eastern and Western cultures. Instead, Western viewers generally consume Korean dramas to understand the characters' behaviors and storylines better from their local perspectives and subjective identities, including race, class perception, gender, and sexuality.

In chapter 4, I analyzed Korean drama viewers on the U.S. Netflix site to show that American viewers were entertained by and engaged with Korean dramas through emotional attachment, much like Asian viewers. These U.S. Netflix viewers presented a similar range of affective modes of reception and earned primarily emotional pleasures while watching Korean dramas. In other words, Korean drama viewers in America responded well to certain levels of similarities or differences regarding lifestyles, personal and social issues, and human relationships within Korean drama narratives. For sure, they perceive that the cultural commonalities in Korean dramas are not necessarily identical to modern Korean culture, but their cultural translations do not heavily rely on ideas of exotic Korean culture or Asian culture. American viewers just naturally absorb this element to make sense of particular cultural accents in Korean dramas, apart from the authentic meanings of their cultural origins.

Based on these findings, cultural hybridity theory does not explain to what extent Korean TV dramas contain a hybrid narrative structure for American viewers or why Korean dramas are less involved in authentic cultural sensibility when received by U.S. viewers. Likewise, this theory is less effective with Western audiences of Korean dramas because their entertainment purposes are less associated with creating a hybrid cultural sphere in between their local world and the imagined Korean drama world. In addition, Korean dramas' storytelling in the narrative and characters is quite distanced from any cultural mixtures. Rather, Korean dramas contain and portray more original and domestic cultural sensibilities that have long been familiar to viewers across the plot, theme, characters, visual images, and life-like episodes. In short, transnational viewers' different viewing experiences of Korean dramas calls for advancing a theoretical model to elaborate the complex meanings of how diverse transnational audiences (including fans) interpret and translate Korean dramas.

Third, the overall transnational flows of Korean TV dramas confirm that the Korean television industry has become part of the global media industry. With the rapid globalization movement, a new international media pecking order has remapped the media and cultural spheres involved in the emergence of new media players, consumer practices, and content flows. An international scope for television programs is no longer the reserve of Western-based conglomerates, and an increasing number of smaller or nation-centric media companies from the developing world continue to expand new paths to international markets. As a consequence, we have seen many diversified media companies at the heart of the transformation of regional media cultures (Chalaby 2016a). Transnational Korean drama is a good example of this living realm of global television. The latest Korean television flows entail not only the flow of various genres and formats, but also the flow of production systems featuring various levels of creativity, human resources, finances, technologies, and commercial abilities. Multidirectional levels of exchange in the transnational television industry pinpoint how the media industry continues to be integrated in a global scale, including countries that had nation-based media systems: active technological convergence, corporate media, and deregulation of media marketplaces all accelerate the global integration of television and other media in different phases.

Once, transnational Korean television studies (along with Korean Wave research) were considered a kind of nationalistic passion, reinforcing the nation's advanced cultural power to the outside, but today Korean television is more connected with both its own region as well as broadened global spaces. Korean television dramas' mobility in crossing these borders is seen in both transnational and transcultural flows, and this book opens up the potential to observe the constant flow of Korean television content in new places around the world. The dissemination of Korean TV dramas is now transgressing cultural, ethnic, and imaginary boundaries beyond the traditional East vs. West division, and transnational viewers' modes of engagement and entertainment practices appear to be quite similar regardless of their cultural territoriality.

Bibliography

ABC Entertainment. 2017. "ABC gives full-season order to TV's no.1 new drama, The Good Doctor." *ABC*, October 3. https://abc.go.com/shows/the-good-doctor/news/updates/abc-gives-full-season-order-to-the-good-doctor.

Ahn, Jungah. 2014. "The new Korean Wave in China: Chinese users' use of Korean popular culture via the Internet." *International Journal of Content* 10 (3): 47–54.

Ainslie, Mary, Sarah D. Lipura, and Joanne B.Y. Lim. 2017. "Understanding the Hallyu backlash in Southeast Asia: A case study of consumers in Thailand, Malaysia and Philippines." *Kritika Kultura* 28: 63–91. http://journals.ateneo.edu/ojs/kk/

Andreeva, Nellie. 2016. "ABC picks up 'Somewhere Between' drama series based on Korean format." *Deadline*, December 16. https://deadline.com/2016/12/abc-somewhere-between-drama-series-korean-format-1201872799/

Andrejevic, Mark. 2008. "Watching television without pity: The productivity of online fans." *Television and New Media* 9 (1): 24–46.

Ang, Ien. 1990. "Culture and communication: Towards an ethnographic critique of media consumption in the transnational media system." *European Journal of Communication* 5: 239–260.

———. 1985. *Watching Dallas: Soap opera and the melodramatic imagination.* London: Methuen.

Artz, Lee. 2015. *Global entertainment media: A critical introduction.* Malden, MA: Wiley Blackwell.

Bai, Ruoyun. 2005. "Media commercialization, entertainment, and the party-state: The political economy of contemporary Chinese television entertainment culture." *Global Media Journal* 4 (6): 1–54.

Bai, Stephany. 2017. "Universal stories help Korean dramas find international success." *NBCnews.com,* January 26.

Barker, Chris. 2002. *Making sense of cultural studies: Central problems and critical debates.* London: Sage.

Beck, Ulrich. (2000) 2003. *What is globalization?* Cambridge: Polity Press.

Baym, Nancy. 2000. *Tune in, log on: Soaps, fandom, and online community.* London: Sage.
Bielby, D. Denis and C. Lee Harrington. 2008. *Global TV: Exporting television and culture in the world market.* New York, NY: NYU Press.
Booth, Paul. 2010. *Digital fandom: New media studies.* New York, NY: Peter Lang.
Booth, Paul and Peter Kelly. 2013. "The changing faces of doctor who fandom: New fans, new technologies, old practices?" *Participations: Journal of Audience & Reception Studies* 10 (1): 56–72.
Brennan, Edward. 2012. "A political economy of formatted pleasures." In *Global television formats: Understanding television across borders*, edited by T. Oren and S. Shahaf, 72–89. New York, NY: Routledge.
Burroughs, Benjamin. 2018. "House of Netflix: Streaming media and digital lore." *Popular Communication.* DOI: 10.1080/15405702.2017.1343948.
Casey, Bernadette, Neil Casey, Ben Calvert, Liam French, and Justin Lewis, eds. 2008. *Television studies: The key concepts* (2nd ed.). London and New York: Routledge.
Chalaby, K. Jean. 2016a. "Television and globalization: The TV content global value chain." *Journal of Communication* 66 (1): 35–59.
———. 2016b. "Drama without drama: The late rise of scripted TV formats." *Television and New Media* 17 (1): 3–20.
———. 2010. "The rise of Britain's super-indies: Policy-making in the age of the global media market." *The International Communication Gazette* 72 (8): 675–693.
Chan, Man Joseph and K.W. Eric Ma. 1996. "Asian television: Global trends and local processes." *International Communication Gazette* 58: 45–60.
Chin, Bertha and H. Lori Morimoto. 2013. "Towards a theory of transcultural fandom." *Participations* 10 (1): 92–108.
Cho, Michelle. 2015. "Meta-Hallyu TV: Global publicity, social media, and the citizen celebrity." In *Hallyu 2.0: The Korean Wave in the age of social media*, edited by S. Lee and A. M. Nornes, 154–171. Ann Arbor, MI: University of Michigan Press.
Cho, Younghan. 2011. "Desperately seeking East Asia amidst the popularity of South Korean pop culture in Asia." *Cultural Studies* 25 (3): 383–404.
Choi, Jeong Bong. 2015. "Loyalty transmission and cultural enlisting of K-pop in Latin America." In *K-pop: The international rise of the Korean music industry*, edited by J. B. Choi and R. Maliangkay, 98–115. New York, NY: Routledge.
Choi, Minjoo. 2018. "Ten Korean TV dramas are remade overseas." *Insight*, May 21. http://www.insight.co.kr/news/155913.
Chua, B. Huat. 2012. *Structure, audience and soft power in East Asian popular culture.* Hong Kong: Hong Kong University Press.
———. 2004. "Conceptualizing an East Asian popular culture." *Inter-Asia Cultural Studies* 5 (2): 200–221.
Chua, B. Huat and Koichi Iwabuchi, eds. 2008. *East Asian pop culture: Analysing the Korean Wave.* Hong Kong: Hong Kong University Press.
Chung, Hye Seung. 2011. "Medium hot, Korean cool: Hallyu envy and reverse mimicry in contemporary U.S. pop culture." In *Hallyu: Influence of Korean popular culture in Asia and beyond*, edited by D. K. Kim and M. Kim, 63–90. Seoul: Seoul National University Press.

Correra, Camille Michell. 2012. "Strong women in the eyes of Filipinas: A reception study of Korean TV dramas." Paper presented at the 6th World Congress of Korean Studies. http://congress.aks.ac.kr/korean/files/2_1357266442.pdf.
Cunningham, Stuart, Elizabeth Jacka, and John Sinclair. 1998. "Global and regional dynamics of international television flows." In *Electronic empires: Global media and local resistance*, edited by D. K. Thussu, 177–192. London: Arnold.
de Castilho, Virgine Borges. 2015. "South Korean pop style: The main aspects of manifestation of Hallyu in South America." *Journal of Sociological Studies* 20: 149–176.
de Certeau, Michel. 1984. *The practice of everyday life*. Berkeley, CA: University of California Press.
du Gay, Paul. 1997. "Introduction." In *Production of culture/cultures of production*, edited by P. du Gay, 1–10. London: Sage.
de Moraes, Lisa. 2018. "Fox's 'The Masked Singer' golden lion terrifies TV critic at TCA." *Deadline, Hollywood*. August 2. https://hollywoodreport.com.
DramaFever.com homepage. https://www.dramafever.com.
DramaFever.com. 2015a. "About Us." http://www.dramafever.com/company/about.html.
———. 2015b. "Affiliates." http://www.dramafever.com/company/affiliates.html.
Elkawy, Amer, Andrey Lekov, Keshab Adhikari, and Miguel Portela. 2015. "Netflix the new face of the TV industry: Entrepreneurship, innovation and business models." https://www.researchgate.net/publication/277311914_Netflix_the_new_face_of_the_TV_industry.
Esser, Andrea. 2010. "Television formats: Primetime staple, global market." *Popular Communication* 8 (4): 273–292.
Fisk, John. 1989. *Understanding popular culture*. Boston, MA: Unwin Hyman.
FRAPA. 2011. "The FRAPA report: Protecting format rights." *The Format Recognition and Protection Association*. https://www.frapa.org/.
FRAPA and B. McKenzie. 2017. "FRAPA legal report 2017: An overview of legal status of formats." *The Format Recognition and Protection Association*.
Fuhr, Michael. 2015. *Globalization and popular music in South Korea: Sounding out K-Pop*. New York, NY: Routledge.
Fujita, Akiko. 2014. "Your next big, addictive TV series could be from South Korea." *PRI's The World*, February 20. https://www.pri.org/stories/2014-02-20/your-next-big-addictive-tv-series-could-be-south-korea.
Glodberg, Lesley. 2016. "Somewhere Between drama ordered straight to series at ABC for summer run." *The Hollywoodreporter*, December 16. https://www.hollywoodreporter.com/live-feed/somewhere-between-drama-ordered-straight-series-at-abc-summer-run-957170.
———. 2014. "ABC adapting hot Korean drama 'My Love From Another Star.'" *The Hollywoodreporter*, September 18. https://www.hollywoodreporter.com/live-feed/my-love-star-abc-remake-733887.
Goldhill, Olivia. 2014. "Netflix announces European expansion plans." *Telegraph*, May 7. http://www.telegraph.co.uk/finance/newsbysector/mediatechnologyandtelecoms/media/10846894/Netflix-announces-European-expansion-plans.html.

Gray, Jonathan. 2003. "New audiences, new textualities: Anti-fans and non-fans." *International Journal of Cultural Studies* 6: 64–81.
Grossberg, Lawrence. 1992. "Is there a fan in the house? The affective sensibility of fandom." In *The adoring audience: Fan culture and popular media*, edited by L.A. Lewis, 50–65. London: Routledge.
Guitton, Julien. 2015. "Netflix: How an 18-year-old company created a new market through the Internet." *E-Commerce and Web Design*. https://www.slideshare.net/JulienGuitton/netflix-case-study-54240175.
Gupta, Akhil and James Ferguson. 1999. "Beyond culture: Space, identity, and the politics of difference." In *Culture, power, place: Explorations in critical anthropology*, edited by A. Gupta and J. Ferguson, 33–51. Durham and London: Duke University Press.
Han, Benjamin. 2017. "K-Pop in Latin America: Transcultural fandom and digital mediation." *International Journal of Communication* 11: 2250–2269.
Hanaki, Toru, Arvind Singhal, Min Wha Han, Do Kyun Kim, and Ketan Chitnis. 2007. "HANRYU sweeps East Asia: How Winter Sonata is gripping Japan." *International Communication Gazette* 69 (3): 281–294.
Harrington, C. Lee and D. Denis Bielby. 2005. "Global television distribution: Implications of TV 'traveling' for viewers, fans, and texts." *American Behavioral Scientist* 48 (7): 902–920.
Haven, Timothy. 2006. *Global television marketplace*. London: Palgrave Macmillan.
Hayashi, Kaori and Eun-Jeung Lee. 2007. "The potential of fandom and the limits of soft power: Media representations on the popularity of a Korean melodrama in Japan." *Social Science Japan Journal* 10 (2): 197–216.
Herreria, Caria. 2017. "Netflix is turning a popular web comic into a Korean drama." *Entertainment*, January 5.
Hilmes, Michelle. 2013. "The whole world's unlikely heroine: Ugly Betty as transnational phenomenon." In *TV's Betty goes global: From telenovela to international brand*, edited by J. McCabe and K. Akass, 26–44. London: I.B. Tauris.
Holiday, Ruth and Joanna Elfving-Hwang. 2012. "Gender, globalization and aesthetic surgery in South Korea." *Body and Society* 18 (2): 58–81.
Hong-Mercier, Seok-Kyeong. 2013. "Hallyu as a digital culture phenomenon in the process of globalization: A theoretical investigation on the global consumption of Hallyu seen in France." *Journal of Communication Research* 50 (1): 157–192.
Hoskins, Colin and Rolf Mirus. 1988. "Reasons for the U.S. dominance of the international trade in television programs." *Media, Culture and Society* 10: 499–515.
Hübinette, Tobias. 2012. "The reception and consumption of Hallyu in Sweden: Preliminary findings and reflections." *Korea Observer* 43 (3): 503–25.
Hukill, A. Mark. 2000. "The politics of television programming in Singapore." In *Television in contemporary Asia*, edited by D. French and M. Richards, 179–196. New Delhi: Sage.
Ish, Kenichi. 1996. "Is the U.S. over-reported in the Japanese press? Factors accounting for international news in the Asahi." *International Communication Gazette* 57: 135–144.
Iwabuchi, Koichi. 2013. "Against banal inter-nationalism." *Asian Journal of Social Science* 41 (5): 437–452.

———. 2008. "Cultures of empire: Transnational media flows and cultural (dis)connections in East Asia." In *Global communications: Toward a transcultural political economy*, edited by P. Chakravartty and Y. Zhao, 143–161. New York, NY: Rowman & Littlefield.

———. 2005. "Discrepant intimacy: Popular culture flows in East Asia." In *Asian media studies*, edited by J.N. Erni and S.K. Chau, 19–36. Malden, MA: Blackwell.

———. 2004a. "Feeling glocal: Japan in the global television format business." In *Television across Asia: Television industries, programme formats and globalization*, edited by Albert Moran and Michael Keane, 21–35. London and New York: Routledge.

———. ed. 2004b. *Feeling Asian modernities: Transnational consumption of Japanese TV dramas*. Hong Kong: Hong Kong University Press.

———. 2002. *Recentering globalization: Popular culture and Japanese transnationalism*. Durham and London: Duke University Press.

Jenkins, Henry. 2004. "The cultural logic of media convergence." *International Journal of Cultural Studies* 7 (1): 33–43.

Jenkins, Henry, Mizuko Ito, and danah boyd. 2016. *Participatory culture in networked era: A conversation on youth, learning, commerce, and politics*. Cambridge and Malden, MA: Polity Press.

Jenner, Mareike. 2017. "Binge-watching: Video-on-demand, quality-TV and mainstreaming fandom." *International Journal of Cultural Studies* 20 (3): 304–320.

Jeon, A-Ram. 2017. "The Good Doctor attracts the United States: Five more episodes add to the first season." *Xportsnews.com*, October 5. http://entertain.naver.com/read?oid=311&aid=0000781199.

Jeon, Jihyun. 2017. "Export Korean TV formats." *MBN News*, August 24. http://news.mk.co.kr/newsRead.php?year=2017&no=568216.

Jeong, Jae-Seon, Seul-Hi Lee, and Sang-Gil Lee. 2017. "When Indonesians routinely consume Korean pop culture: Revisiting Jakartan fans of the Korean drama Dae Jang Geum." *International Journal of Communication* 11: 2288–2307.

Jeong, Jong-Ho. 2012. "Ethnoscapes, mediascapes, and ideoscapes: Socio-cultural relations between South Korea and China." *Journal of International and Area Studies* 19 (2): 77–95.

Jin, Dal Yong. 2016. *New Korean Wave: Transnational cultural power in the age of social media*. Chicago, IL: University of Illinois Press.

Jin, Dal Yong and Kyong Yoon. 2016. "The social mediascape of transnational Korean pop culture: Hallyu 2.0 as spreadable media practice." *New Media and Society* 18 (7): 1277–1292.

Joo, Moonjung. 2016. "The two Korean TV dramas rewrite the history of Korean Wave in the US." *EtNews*, February 6. http://www.etnews.com/20160206000069.

Ju, Hyejung. 2019. "Korean TV drama viewership on Netflix: Transcultural affection, romance, and identities." *Journal of International and Intercultural Communication*, Doi:10.1080/17513057.2019.1606269.

———. 2017. "National television moves to the region and beyond: South Korean TV drama production with a new cultural act." *Journal of International Communication* 23 (1): 94–114.

———. 2014. "Transformations of the Korean media industry by the Korean Wave: The perspective of glocalization." In *The Korean Wave: Korean popular culture in global context*, edited by Y. Kuwahara, 33–52. New York, NY: Palgrave Macmillan.
Ju, Hyejung and Soobum Lee. 2015. "The Korean Wave and Asian Americans: The ethnic meanings of transnational Korean pop culture in the USA." *Continuum: Journal of Media & Cultural Studies* 29 (3): 323–338.
Jung, Eun-Young. 2009. "Transnational Korea: A critical assessment of the Korean Wave in Asia and the United States." *Southeast Review of Asian Studies* 31: 69–80.
Jung, Sun. 2013. "K-pop beyond Asia: Performing trans-nationality, trans-industriality, and trans-textuality." In *Asian popular culture in transition*, edited by J. A. Lent and L. Fitzsimmons, 108–130. New York, NY: Routledge.
———. 2011a. "K-pop, Indonesian fandom, and social media." *Transformative Works and Cultures* 8: 1–22.
———. 2011b. *Korean masculinities and transcultural consumption: Yonsama, Rain, Oldboy, K-pop idols*. Hong Kong: Hong Kong University Press.
———. 2009. "A study on the operation improvement plans for a special purpose company." (Report No. 2009–27). Seoul: Korea Culture and Tourism Institute.
Kang, John. 2016. "Korean drama 'Descendants of the Sun' breaks records thanks to Chinese investments." *Forbes [Asia]*, April 5.
Kaplan, Andreas and Michael Haenlein. 2010. "Users of the world, Unite! The challenges and opportunities of social media." *Business Horizons* 53 (1): 59–68.
Keane, Michael. 2008. "From national preoccupation to overseas aspirati-on." In *TV drama in China: Unfolding Narratives of tradition, political transformation and Cosmopolitan identity*, edited by Ying Zhu, Michael K-eane, and Ruoyun Bai, 1–17. Hong Kong: Hong Kong University Press.
Keane, Michael, Anthony Y.H. Fung, and Albert Moran. 2007. *New television, globalization, and the East Asian cultural imagination*. Hong Kong: Hong Kong University Press.
Keane, Michael and Bonnie Rui Liu. 2013. "China's new creative strategy: The utilization of cultural soft power and new markets." In *Asian popular culture: The global (dis)continuity*, edited by Anthony Y. H. Fung, 233–249. London: Routledge.
Kibria, Nazli. 2003. *Becoming Asian American: Second-generation Chinese and Korean American identities*. Baltimore, MD: Johns Hopkins University Press.
Kil, Sonia. 2017. "Netflix sets 'Love Alarm' as its first original Korean Drama." *Variety*, January 4.
Kim, Bok-rae. 2015. "Past, present and future of Hallyu (Korean Wave)." *American International Journal of Contemporary Research* 5 (5): 154–160.
Kim, Do Kyun. 2011. "A comparative study between Hallyu and Telenovela: Strategies for media globalization." In *Hallyu: Influence of Korean popular culture in Asia and beyond*, edited by D. K. Kim and M. Kim, 369–397. Seoul: Seoul National University Press.
Kim, Yeo-Ri. 2017. "The first U.S. remake of a Korean drama debuts this summer." *Huffpost*, August 10. https://www.huffingtonpost.com/entry/the-first-us-remake-of-a-korean-drama-debuts-this-summer_us_598c6ea6e4b030f0e267ca54.
Kim, Youna, ed. 2013. *The Korean Wave: Korean media go global*. London and New York: Routledge.

Korea Communication Commission. 2006. *Broadcasting industry white paper*. Seoul, Korea: KCC.
———. 2005. *Broadcasting industry white paper*. Seoul, Korea: KCC.
———. 2004. *Broadcasting industry white paper*. Seoul, Korea: KCC.
Korea Creative Content Agency. 2015. *Content industry statistics*. Naju, Korea: KOCCA.
———. 2014a. *Content industry statistics*. Naju, Korea: KOCCA.
———. 2014b. *Strategic plans of Korean TV format export and localization*. Naju, Korea: KOCCA.
———. 2011. *Broadcasting contents format industry report*. Seoul, Korea: KOCCA.
Kraidy, M. Marwan. 2005. *Hybridity or the cultural logic of globalization*. Philadelphia, PA: Temple University Press.
Kustritz, Anne. 2015. "Transnationalism, localization, and translation in European fandom: Fan studies as global media and audience studies." *Transformative Works and Cultures* 19. http://dx.doi.org/10.3983/twc.2015.0682.
Latour, Bruno. 2005. *Reassembling the social: An introduction to actor-network theory*. Oxford and New York: Oxford University Press.
Lee, S. Claire and Yasue Kuwahara. 2014. "'Gangnam Style' as format: When a localized Korean song meets a global audience." In *The Korean Wave: Korean popular culture in global context*, edited by Y. Kuwahara, 101–116. New York, NY: Palgrave Macmillan.
Lee, Dong-Hoo. 2008. "Popular cultural capital and cultural identity: Young Korean women's cultural appropriation of Japanese TV dramas." In *East Asian pop culture: Analysing the Korean Wave*, edited by B. H. Chua and K. Iwabuchi, 157–172. Hong Kong: Hong Kong University Press.
———. 2004. "Cultural contact with Japanese TV dramas: Modes of reception and narrative transparency." In *Feeling Asian modernities: Transnational consumption of Japanese TV dramas*, edited by K. Iwabuchi, 251–274. Hong Kong: Hong Kong University Press.
Lee, Hyo-won. 2014. "Hit South Korean TV shows to get China, Southeast Asia remakes." *Hollywoodreporter.com*, March 26. https://www.hollywoodreporter.com/news/hit-south-korean-tv-shows-691262.
Lee, Hyo-won and Georg Szalai. 2016. "U.S., Europe looking to catch Korean TV drama wave." *Hollywoodreporter.com*, April 5. http://www.hollywoodreporter.com/news/korean-tv-dramas-us-eruope=879850.
Lee, Min-hung and Yoo-chul Kim. 2016. "Netflix keen on Korean dramas and movies." *Korea Times*, January 10. http://www.koreatimes.co.kr/www/common/printpreview.asp?categoryCode=133&newsIdx=195083.
Lee, Sangjoon. 2015. "From diaspora TV to social media: Korean TV dramas in America." In *Hallyu 2.0: The Korean Wave in the age of social media*, edited by S. Lee and A. M. Nornes, 172–191. Ann Arbor, MI: University of Michigan Press.
Lee, Soobum and Hyejung Ju. 2010. "Korean television dramas in Japan: Imagining *East Asianness* and consuming *nostalgia*." *Asian Women*, 26 (2): 77–105.
Lie, John. 2012. "What is the K in K-pop?" *Korean Observer* 43 (3): 339–363.

Lim, Louisa. 2006. "South Korean culture wave spreads across Asia." *National Public Radio*, March 26. https://www.npr.org/templates/story/story.php?storyId=5 300970.

Lin, Aagel and Avin Tong. 2008. "Re-imagining a cosmopolitan 'Asian Us': Korean media flows and imaginaries of Asian modern femininities." In *East Asian pop culture: Analysing the Korean Wave*, edited by B. H. Chua and K. Iwabuchi, 91–125. Hong Kong: Hong Kong University Press.

Lobato, Ramon. 2018. "Rethinking international TV flows research in the age of Netflix." *Television and New Media* 19 (3): 241–256.

———. 2016. "The cultural logic of digital intermediaries: YouTube multichannel networks." *Convergence: The International Journal of Research into New Media Technologies* 22 (4): 348–360.

Madrid-Morales, Dani and Bruno Lovric. 2015. "Transatlantic connection: K-pop and K-drama fandom in Spain and Latin America." *Journal of Fandom Studies* 3 (1): 23–41.

Mai, Nicola and Russell King. 2009. "Love, sexuality and migration: Mapping the issue(s)." *Mobilities* 4 (3): 295–307.

McDonald, Kevin and Daniel Smith-Rowsey, eds. 2016. *The Netflix effect: Technology and entertainment in the 21st century*. New York and London: Bloomsbury.

Mikos, Lothar. 2016. "Digital media platforms and the use of TV content: Binge watching and video-on-demand in Germany." *Media and Communication* 4 (3): 154–161.

Ministry of Culture, Sports, and Tourism. 2012. *Broadcasting industry white paper*. Seoul, Korea: MCST.

———. 2011. *Broadcasting industry white paper*. Seoul, Korea: MCST.

———. 2010. *Broadcasting industry white paper*. Seoul, Korea: MCST.

Ministry of Science, ICT and Future Planning. 2016. *Broadcasting industry report*. Seoul, Korea: MSIF.

———. 2014. *Broadcasting industry report*. Seoul, Korea: MSIF.

———. 2013. *Broadcasting industry report*. Seoul, Korea: MSIF.

Mittell, Jason. 2015. *Complex TV: The poetics of contemporary television storytelling*. New York, NY: New York University Press.

Molen, Sherri L. Ter. 2014. "A cultural imperialistic homecoming: The Korean Wave reaches the United States." In *The Korean Wave: Korean popular culture in global context*, edited by Y. Kuwahara, 149–187. New York: Palgrave Macmillan.

Moran, Albert. 2004. "Television formats in the world/the world of television formats." In *Television across Asia: Television industries, programme formats and globalization*, edited by A. Moran and M. Keane, 1–8. London and New York: Routledge.

Moran, Albert and Michael Keane, eds. 2004. *Television across Asia: Television industries, programme formats and globalization*. London and New York: Routledge.

Moran, Albert and Justin Malbon. 2006. *Understanding the global TV format*. Bristol: Intellect.

Morley, David. 2006. "Globalisation and cultural imperialism reconsidered: Old questions in new guises." In *Media and cultural theory*, edited by J. Curran and D. Morley, 30–43. New York, NY: Routledge.

———. 1992. *Television, audience and cultural studies*. London: Routledge.

Negus, Keith. 2002. "The work of cultural intermediaries and the enduring distance between production and consumption." *Cultural Studies* 16 (4): 501–515.

Netflix. 2018. https://media.netflix.com/en/press-releases.

Nikunen, Kaarina. 2007. "The intermedial practices of fandom." *Nordicom Review* 28 (2): 111–128.

Novak, N. Alison. 2016. "Framing the future of media regulation through Netflix." In *The Netflix effect: Technology and entertainment in the 21st century*, edited by K. McDonald and D. Smith-Rowsey, 33–47. New York and London: Bloomsbury.

Oba, Goro and M. Sylvia Chan-Olmsted. 2005. "The development of cable television in East Asian countries: A comparative analysis of determinants." *International Communication Gazette* 67: 211–237.

Oh, Chuyun. 2014. "The politics of the dancing body: Racialized and gendered femininity in Korean pop." In *The Korean Wave: Korean popular culture in global context*, edited by Y. Kuwahara, 53–81. New York, NY: Palgrave Macmillan.

Oh, Miyoung. 2014. "An exploratory study on the Korean Wave in the U.S.: Focusing on in-depth interviews of Korean language exchange meet-up members." [In Korean] *The Journal of Media Economy and Culture* 12 (3): 46–92.

Oh, Youjeong. 2015. "The interactive nature of Korean TV dramas: Flexible texts, discursive consumption, and social media." In *Hallyu 2.0: The Korean Wave in the age of social media*, edited by S. Lee and A. M. Nornes, 133–153. Ann Arbor, MI: University of Michigan Press.

Onishi, Norimitsu. 2006. "China's youth look to Seoul for inspiration." The *New York Times*, January 2. http://web.lexis-nexis.com.

Otmazgin, Nissim and Irina Lyan. 2013. "Hallyu across the desert: K-pop fandom in Israel and Palestine." *Cross-Currents: East Asian History and Cultural Review* 9: 68–89.

Park, Susun. 2013. "Korean drama production has to be reformed." *PD Journal*, July 26. http://www.pdjournal.com/news/articlePrint.html?idxno=39235.

Russell, Mark, and George Wehrfritz. 2004. ''Blockbuster nation: How Seoul beat Hollywood, making Korea an Asian Star.'' *Newsweek*, May 4. http://www.newsweek.com/2004/05/02/blockbuster-nation.htmli.

Ryoo, Woongjae. 2009. "Globalization, or the logic of cultural hybridization: The case of the Korean Wave." *Asian Journal of Communication* 19 (2): 137–151.

Schulze, Marion. 2013. "Korea vs. K-dramaland: The culturalization of K-dramas by international fans." *Acta Koreana* 16 (2): 367–397.

Shi, Yu. 2005. "Identity construction of the Chinese diaspora, ethnic media use, community formation, and the possibility of social activism." *Continuum: Journal of Media & Cultural Studies* 19 (2): 55–72.

Shim, Doobo. 2006. "Hybridity and the rise of Korean popular culture in Asia." *Journal of Media, Culture and Society* 28 (1): 25–44.

Shim, Doobo and Dal Yong Jin. 2007. "Transformations and development of the Korean broadcasting media." In *Negotiating democracy: Media transformations in emerging democracies*, edited by I. A. Blankson and P. D. Murphy, 161–176. New York, NY: State University of New York Press.

Sinclair, John. 1996a. "Mexico, Brazil, and the Latin world." In *New patterns in global television: Peripheral vision*, edited by J. Sinclair, E. Jacka, and S. Cunningham, 33–66. Oxford: Oxford University Press.

———. 1996b. "Culture and trade: Some theoretical and practical considerations." In *Mass media and free trade: NAFTA and the cultural industries*, edited by E.G. McAnany and K. T. Wilkinson, 30–60. Austin, TX: University of Texas Press.
Sohn, Ji-young. 2018. "Netflix to push boundaries of Korean media content." *The Korea Herald*, January 25.
Song, Bomi. 2016. "The syndrome of descendants of the Sun." *Economic Review*, March 28. http://m.post.naver.com/viewer/postView.nhn?volumeNo=3898838&memberNo=11292208&vType=VERTICAL.
Straubhaar, Joseph. 1996. "Distinguishing the global, regional and national levels of world television." In *Media in global context: A reader*, edited by A. Sreberny-Mohammadi et al., 284–298. London and New York: Arnold.
———. 1991. "Beyond media imperialism: Asymmetrical interdependence and cultural proximity." *Critical Studies in Mass Communication* 8: 39–59.
Steemers, Jeanette, Petros Isoifidis, and Mark Wheeler. 2005. *European television industries*. London: BFI.
Sung, Sang-Yeon. 2013. "K-pop reception and participatory fan culture in Austria." *Cross-Currents: East Asian History and Culture Review* 9: 90–104.
Tan, Huileng. 2017. "Netflix bet on Korean drama for expansion." *CNBC*, January 9.
Thornton, Niamh. 2010. "YouTube: Transnational fandom and Mexican divas." *Transnational Cinemas* 1 (1): 53–67.
Thussu, Daya. 2007. *Media on the move: Global flow and contra-flow*. London: Routledge.
Trivedi, Anjani. 2013. "Forget politics, let's dance: Why K-Pop is a Latin American smash." *Time*, August 1. http://world.time.com/2013/08/01/forget-politics-lets-dance-why-k-pop-is-a-latin-american-smash/.
Tryon, Chuck. 2015. "TV got better: Netflix's original programming strategies and binge viewing." *Media Industries Journal* 2 (2): 104–16.
Tunstall, Jeremy. 2008. *The media were American: U.S. mass media in decline*. New York and Oxford: Oxford University Press.
TVN drama homepage. http://program.tving.com/tvn/signal.
van Zoonen, Liesbet. 2001. "Desire and resistance: *Big Brother* and the recognition of everyday life." *Media, Culture, and Society* 23: 669–677.
Wagmeister, Elizabeth. 2016. "ABC greenlights murder mystery 'Somewhere Between' with 10-episode order for Summer 2017." *Variety*, December 16. https://variety.com/2016/tv/news/abc-somewhere-between-series-1201944513/.
Wang, Jing. 2001. "Culture as leisure and culture as capital." *Positions* 9 (1): 69–104.
West, Kelly. 2013. "Unsurprising: Netflix survey indicates people like to binge-watch TV." *Cinemablend.com*. December 13. https://www.cinemablend.com/television/Unsurprising-Netflix-Survey-Indicates-People-Like-Binge-Watch-TV-61045.html.
White, Mimi. 2003. "Flows and other close encounters with television." In *Planet TV: A global television reader*, edited by L. Parks and S. Kumar, 94–110. New York: New York University Press.
White, Peter. 2013. "UK Indies storm US upfronts." *Broadcast*, April 4. https://www.broadcastnow.co.uk/uk-indies-storm-us-upfronts/5053547.article.

Wong, Tessa. 2016. "Descendants of the Sun: The Korean military romance sweeping Asia." *BBC News [Asia]*, March 27.
Wong, Wailin. 2010. "Korean TV dramas find new fans, outlets with online video: DramaFever Web site delivers shows via Hulu." *Chicago Tribune*, May 17. http://articles.chicagotribune.com/2010-05-17/business/ct-biz-0517-koreandramas--20100517_1_online-video-korean-tv-dramas.
Yang, Eun-kyeong. 2003. "The circulation of East Asian trendy dramas grounded on cultural proximity." [In Korean] *Broadcasting Research* 69: 197–220.
Yang, Irene Fang-Chih. 2008. "Engaging with Korean dramas: Discourses of gender, media, and class formation in Taiwan." *Asian Journal of Communication* 18 (1): 64–79.
Yang, Jonghoe. 2012. "The Korean Wave (Hallyu) in East Asia: A comparison of Chinese, Japanese, and Taiwanese audiences who watch Korean TV dramas." *Development and Society* 41 (1): 103–147.
Yasumoto, Seiko. 2014. "Popular culture: Islands of fandom in East Asia." *The IAFOR Journal of Asian Studies* 1 (1): 1–15.
Yecise, Brian. 2016. "The Chinese-Korean co-production pact: Collaborative encounters and the accelerating expansion of Chinese cinema." *The International Journal of Cultural Policy* 22 (5): 770–786.
Yin, Fu Su Kelly. 2005. "Hallyu in Singapore: Korean consumerism or the consumption of Chineseness?" *Korea Journal* 45 (4): 206–232.
Yoo, Sekyong and Kyeong-Sook Lee. 2001. "Cultural proximity among East Asian countries' television dramas." *Korean Journal of Journalism and Communication Studies* 45 (3): 230–267.
Yoon, Goeun. 2018, "A Korean Odyssey can't be postponed under contract with Netflix: Netflix invests the Korean broadcasting industry." *Yonhapnews*, January 18. http://www.yonhapnews.co.kr/dev/9601000000.html.
Yoon, Kyong. 2017. "Cultural translation of K-Pop among Asian Canadian fans." *International Journal of Communication* 11: 2350–2366.
Yoon, Kyong and Dal Yong Jin. 2016. "The Korean wave phenomenon in Asian diasporas in Canada." *Journal of Intercultural Studies* 37 (1): 69–83.
Yoshino, Kosaku. 1999. "Rethinking theories of nationalism: Japan's nationalism in a marketplace perspective." In *Consuming ethnicity and nationalism: Asian experiences*, edited by K. Yoshino, 8–28. Honolulu, HI: University of Hawai'i Press.
Yu, Konshik and Sanghyun Moon. 2014. "Special purpose company and drama production: A case study of KGCS." *The Korea Contents Society* 14 (2): 172–180.
Yu, Roger. 2013. "American audiences: I want my international TV." *USA Today*, March 21.
Yu, S. Sherry. 2015. "The inevitably dialectic nature of ethnic media." *Global Media Journal: Canadian Edition* 8 (2): 133–140.

Index

ABC, 24, 99, 100, 104
advertising-based profit making model, 23, 50
affective affinity, 69, 71, 113
asymmetric inter-Asian media flows, 10

BBC, 16, 23, 84
binge-watching, 71–72
Boys Over Flowers, 34, 48–49, 91

center-peripheral media flow, 12
China Central Television (CCTV), 18, 50
CJ E&M, 25, 91, 109–10
class hierarchy, 40, 47
Comprehensive TV channels, 24, 26n4, 90
contraflow, 2
coproduction, 46, 51–52, 56–59, 109
copyright, 84, 90, 98
cultural discount, 21, 22, 26n2
cultural proximity (cultural affinity), 10–11, 85–86, 93n2
cultural repertoire, 35, 86

Descendants of the Sun, 25, 52–54, 90
DramaFever.com, 25, 33, 49, 83, 85, 91–93, 113
dual production system, 23

fandom, 35, 41, 69, 71, 73, 75–76, 82, 91, 113
format, 13, 47, 49, 56, 59, 95, 97–100, 102–3, 108–9, 115
Format Recognition and Protection Association (FRAPA), 98

Go Back Couple, 36–37
Goblin, 33, 90, 93

Hallyu, 9, 55; Hallyu 1.0, 16, 23; Hallyu 2.0, 16, 27
Heirs, 34, 42, 49, 92
Hulu, 25, 83, 92

idol bands, 16, 25n1
independent TV production company(studio), 22–23, 52, 58, 100
inter-Asian media flow, 10, 47, 86
intermediary consumption, 41, 49, 85
intertextual reading, 34, 41
IQiyi, 25, 51–52, 54

Japanese Wave, 15
joint venture, 46, 51, 57, 109
JTBC, 24, 90, 91, 101, 110

Korean Broadcasting System (KBS), 18, 22–24, 37, 43n2, 48, 53, 91, 100

Korean TV drama (K-drama), 16–17, 27, 46, 50, 55, 65, 69, 77, 81, 85, 88, 112; broadcast rights, 25, 51, 57; celebrities, 23, 43n2, 49, 54, 58; foreign TV quota, 50, 54; K-dramaland, 42; production, 32, 49, 52–53, 59, 115; romance narrative, 30, 32–35, 37, 49, 56, 77
Korean Wave, 9, 15, 27, 45, 50, 55, 81, 84, 88, 102, 112
K-pop, 16, 46, 80, 84, 85

Man To Man, 25, 90
mediascape, 64, 80
Meteor Garden, 47, 49
MIP-TV, 56, 110
Mr. Sunshine, 25, 90
Munwha Broadcast Corporation (MBC), 22, 23, 25, 57, 91, 100

narrative complexity, 28–29, 32, 67
nationalism, 14–15, 115–16
nation-sponsored media model, 14
NBC, 24, 108
neoliberal globalization, 12, 15
Netflix, 24–25, 32, 65, 67, 70, 76, 81, 83, 85, 87–91, 103, 113
network TV, 22, 24, 53, 90, 91, 98, 103, 109–110
NHK, 24, 57

OCN, 24, 90, 100
ordorless, 15

parasocial interaction, 70–71, 76

paratextual activities (practices), 41, 42n1
pecking order, 3, 14, 115
pop cosmopolitanism, 64
production bible, 97–98, 108

remake, 48–49, 56, 98, 102, 104
Reply series, 24

Secret Garden, 38, 73
Seoul Broadcasting System (SBS), 22, 24–25, 59, 91, 100, 102
Signal, 24, 94n3, 102
social media, 41, 64, 79, 82
soft masculinity, 37–39
soft power, 80, 112
special production company (SPC), 53, 57
storytelling mode, 28–30, 34, 36, 113, 115
streaming, 24–25, 49, 51–52, 64–65, 80, 83, 85, 103, 113
Studio Dragon, 25

telenovela, 22, 28, 72, 81, 92, 93n1, 99
translatability, 28, 35
transnational media flow(s), 27, 50, 64, 75, 81, 111
TVN, 24–25, 71, 90, 92, 101

Viki.com, 85

Winter Sonata, 24, 42, 43n2, 55

YouKu, 25, 51–52

About the Author

Hyejung Ju is an associate professor of mass communication at Claflin University (South Carolina, United States). Dr. Ju teaches media studies courses regarding broadcast media, digital media culture, and audiences in global media contexts. She has researched on transnational television industries, audience cultures, and the impact of global and digital media environments, especially focusing on the distribution and consumption of non-Western television content. For years, she has published scholarly articles in several journals, including *Journal of International & Intercultural Communication*, *Journal of International Communication*, *Continuum: Journal of Media & Cultural Studies*, *Asian Women*, *Communication, Culture, & Critique*, and *Oxford Research Encyclopedia of Communication*. In tandem with the Korean Wave phenomena, she contributed her chapters in the two edited books, entitled *The Korean Wave: Korean Popular Culture in Global Context (2014)*, and *Hallyu: Influence of Korean Popular Culture in Asia and Beyond (2011)*.

www.ingramcontent.com/pod-product-compliance
Lightning Source LLC
Chambersburg PA
CBHW050910300426
44111CB00010B/1459